WOMEN TAKE CARE

WOMEN

The Consequences of

With the Older Women's League
Task Force on Caregivers
and
Judy MacLean, Consulting Writer

TRIAD PUBLISHING COMPANY

TAKE CARE

Caregiving in Today's Society

Tish Sommers

Laurie Shields

GAINESVILLE, FLORIDA

Library of Congress Cataloging-in-Publication Data

Sommers, Tish.
  Women take care.

  Bibliography: p.
  1. Handicapped--United States--Care--Case studies.
2. Aged--United States--Care--Case studies. 3. Helping
behavior--Case studies. 4. Aged women--United States--
Psychology--Case studies. I. Shields, Laurie.
II. Older Women's League (U.S.). Task Force on
Caregivers. III. Title.
HV1553.S64 1987   649.8   87-25465
ISBN 0-937404-28-4
ISBN 0-937404-27-6 (pbk.)

For information regarding quantity orders, contact Special Sales Department,
Triad Publishing Company, 1110 NW 8th Avenue, Gainesville, FL 32601.

For information about the Older Women's League (OWL), write Older Women's
League, 730 11th Street NW, Suite 300, Washington, DC 20001.

Cover credits:
Photo-mosaics by Michael Rubin
Design by Paul E. Newman

Contributors

Donna Ambrogi is coordinator of the Older Women's League Task Force on Caregivers and directing attorney of the California Law Center on Long Term Care.

Margaret Baker-Riley, MA, MPH, is a doctoral candidate in public health at the University of California, Berkeley, doing research on paid caregivers.

Linda Crossman, RN, MS, is Executive Director, Marin Adult Day Health Services, San Anselmo, California. She serves on the National Advisory Committee, National Council on Aging Family Caregivers Project, Washington, DC.

Lynn Gigy, PhD in human development and aging, has done research on issues of aging and caregivers.

Eugenia Hickman is a retired social worker, co-founder of over sixty clinics, caregiver for her parents, and an advocate for training and licensing of caregivers.

Kathleen Kelly, MPA, is manager of services and education programs at Family Survival Project, San Francisco, a caregiver support organization.

CONTRIBUTORS

Frances Leonard is legal counsel of the Older Women's League.

Cecilia London, LCSW, is the supervisor of geriatric services, Jewish Family and Children Services of San Francisco. She is a past and current caregiver support group leader.

Claudio Luna, MSW, is a geriatric social worker, Catholic Charities of San Francisco.

Judy MacLean is a freelance writer and editor.

Alice Quinlan is the Director of Public Policy, Older Women's League.

Ida VSW Red, MSLS, is the Resource Director, Institute for Health & Aging, University of California, San Francisco, and is published in several lesbian anthologies.

Laurie Shields is co-founder of the Older Women's League.

Dorothy Smith is a former primary caregiver for her parents. She and her mother, Dolores Wilson, publish CROSSROADS, a periodical dealing with issues of concern to women.

Tish Sommers (1914-1985) was co-founder of the Older Women's League.

Rinna Evelyn Wolfe is a single, career woman, an educator and writer. As the eldest daughter in her family, she was responsible for secondary care of two parents in a nursing home.

To Clemmie Barry
1901 - 1985

Who recognized the caregiver's need for special support services and whose eloquent presentations at the founding of the Older Women's League in 1980 led to national action on the issue and, ultimately, to the writing of this book.

Contents

9

Foreword

In 1982, thirteen people were asked to serve on the Older Women's League National Task Force on Caregivers. They met and, without remuneration, began work on this book.

Providing expertise in many areas, each of the contributing authors also critiqued one another's work. The result of this truly collaborative labor of love was skillfully woven together by consulting writer, Judy MacLean, with the assistance of Laurie Shields and Donna Ambrogi, chair of the Task Force. By mutual agreement, all royalties from the sale of *Women Take Care* will accrue to the general support of the Older Women's League.

In addition to Tish Sommers and Laurie Shields, the contributing authors are (in alphabetical order) Donna Ambrogi, Margaret Baker-Riley, Linda Crossman, Lynn Gigy, Eugenia Hickman, Kathy Kelly, Fran Leonard, Cecilia London, Dorothy Smith, and Rinna Evelyn Wolfe. Thanks are due to Judy MacLean, consulting writer, to Ida VSW Red, for writing the Resource chapter, to Claudio Luna and Alice Quinlan for their assistance on the final drafts, and to Margaret Malberti, for preparing the manuscript. Finally, thanks are due to the San Francisco Foundation for a grant that helped to fund the research and writing.

WASHINGTON, DC   LOU GLASSE, PRESIDENT
1986   OLDER WOMEN'S LEAGUE

11

Introduction

"I am a survivor of seventeen years of caretaking of my husband. And now, after forty years of marriage, I have had to give in to letting him go into a nursing home because there was no adequate respite care nor relief from my 24-hours-a-day duty. I have decided there must be a change . . . that we, the wives, can no longer be ignored."

Clemmie Barry was born in 1901 and raised on a Nebraska farm. Always concerned with social injustice, she acted upon her convictions more than most. As a young woman she organized hosiery workers in Parkersburg, West Virginia and in 1934 joined in the big union drive in the south under the auspices of the Amalgamated Clothing Workers. Fired for union activity, she became a defendent in a famous test case of labor law under the newly formed National Labor Relations Board (NLRB). Four years later she married another fighter for social causes, Dick Barry. Together they battled for the larger liberal issues of their day—the cause of labor, the defeat of fascism, and the rights of black people to live where they pleased.

Then Dick Barry had a stroke in 1960 and the life of this activist couple changed drastically. Clemmie was 59 years old at the time. For the next seventeen years she took care of Dick full-time, until her own health failed. "I felt like I had betrayed my trust to him when I finally had to place him. We had always been such a strong team and now I was letting my side down. Although he never expressed it, I thought that he must feel deserted."

But Clemmie was an organizer. She knew from experience that the isolation, the frustration, and the guilt that she experienced were not hers alone and were shared by other women in her situation. Despite all the social programs developed in the 1960s and '70s, the lonely plight of the caregiver was largely invisible. So after Dick was placed in a nursing home, Clemmie Barry organized a group of women like herself. It was called "Women Who Care." This support group for women caregivers in Marin County, California, was one of the first in the United States.

In her letter reaching out to found it, she wrote: "I believe that we can build support among ourselves as a group. I am willing to be the focal point for such an undertaking. If this can come about I would hope that we might create an atmosphere among ourselves where the unshed tears, the too long contained grief, and yes, even the anger and frustration might find an outlet. That no one would give advice, nor make judgments. Personal decisions and solutions must come out of each person's own understanding of her need. First, I would hope that there might be immediate help, just in the sharing. Then I would hope that we could collectively find our voice and make it heard among the legislators."

In October, 1980, two years after Dick Barry's death, Clemmie attended the White House Mini-Conference on Older Women because she felt the plight of caregivers should be brought to public attention. She told the 400 women and a few men in Des Moines, Iowa, what it means to be tied day and night to another human being—no matter how much you love him—with no prospect of change except the gradual deterioration of a husband and eventual widowhood. She talked about the need for someone to take over from time to time to give the caregiver a break, and the need for other support services to make the burden more tolerable, to allow a woman who works as a non-paid caregiver to retain a little of her freedom. The conference strongly supported her.

That was the beginning. The Older Women's League (OWL) was formed, the day following the conference, to bring the invisible problems women face in their later years to public attention and to work toward their solution. Since the need was great, OWL grew rapidly, with chapters springing up across the country within a year. A "gray paper" on the topic "Til Death Do Us Part: Caregiving Wives of Severely Disabled Husbands," was published by OWL. It was based on interviews of women in this situation and discussions with OWL members who understood the legal and legislative aspects of the problem. This led to greater recognition by OWL members of how the caregiver problem touches most women's lives in one way or another. An OWL Task Force on Caregivers was formed in February, 1982, to prepare a model state respite care bill. This legislation was the opening wedge to begin advocacy for caregivers, to make women more aware of the problem and to open up the plight of the caregiver to media attention. Unless a woman's problem is brought to public attention, it can remain a festering sore with no effort made at healing. Clemmie Barry's initiative had taken root.

A Woman's Issue

Who are the caregivers of disabled adults? It will come as no surprise to learn that approximately three-fourths or more are female. Women are the primary caregivers of young children, and as our society ages, more and more women will find themselves back on this job. Women are presumed to be responsible for the well-being of their family members and until quite recently, the care and well-being of the family was the only occupation of a large percentage of women in this country. For those who also worked outside the home, including many lower-income women, family caregiving was an additional responsibility. In the recent past, the spinster daughter was the expected caregiver of a widowed aging parent. Today, primary caregivers in family settings are overwhelmingly spouses and daughters, and then sisters, daughters-in-law, nieces, and friends. Concern for the caregiver is very much a woman's issue.

Of course, some men are very effective caregivers. Husbands who find themselves in the position of providing "hands on" care of a wife with a crippling disease like a stroke or multiple sclerosis (which strikes females much more frequently than males) experience the same pressures. Sons often contribute to the care of parents (though usually not full-time) or they provide a paid surrogate. Some men in a situation of responsibility for a disabled adult take on the task with the same dedication as women. But this situation occurs far less frequently for males than females, because it is a role reversal. For women, caregiving is an expected duty; for men, it is an unexpected expression of compassion. One man interviewed said explicitly, "Men just don't have the knack for caring for the sick and dying." "The knack" may be a lifetime of social expectations.

The term *caregiver*, as we are using it here, covers a wide spectrum of services, depending on the degree of disability, living arrangements and economic circumstances. It can range from time-consuming support and attention of a daughter or son for a widowed mother in a nursing home, to the 24-hour home care of an ailing spouse. There may or may not be outside help. Very frequently, as the disability increases, there is a progression from sporadic chores to round-the-clock care. This is particularly true in the dementing illnesses like Alzheimer's disease, which afflicts over one million older adults in the United States.

Women are susceptible to what has rightly been called by feminists "the compassion trap." Those very nurturing skills and sensitivity to human interactions that make women as a sex more responsive to pain and suffering also make us more willing to take on arduous and often unrewarded personal duties. The

16

rewards are seen as "feeling useful" or "making a difference." Compassion is in too short supply for society to lose any of it. The question is, can women as individuals provide all the compassion needed, especially as the population ages and chronic illness becomes even more common than it is today? What are the responsibilities of a compassionate society?

The phenomenon of greater longevity is a mixed blessing both for the aged and for those who care for them in their declining years. The medical profession has been more successful in keeping people alive than in making them well. As matters now stand, society is counting on women to bear the largest part of the burden of caring for family members who can no longer care for themselves. Compassionate women may find the pressures unbearable, unless the burden is shared more equitably.

The duty of caring for failing elderly relatives is more than a family matter, a personal dilemma, or a sex equity issue. Basically, it is a problem of how our society views old and disabled people. With the growing numbers of chronically ill, it can no longer be a matter of "out of sight, out of mind." It can no longer be some other family's tragedy. Eventually we must face hard questions, as individuals and as a nation.

Who is responsible for long term care? Who will pay for it? What is the most humane way to care for a dying person suffering from cancer, stroke, Alzheimer's disease, Parkinson's disease, or any of the other debilitating and crippling illnesses that plague an aging population? And who will provide the day-and-night attendance that is often needed? If these questions are not resolved, most of us will one day find ourselves in a situation we never thought about or planned for. Whatever we do will never seem adequate, and we will be riddled with guilt.

The women's movement has examined many of the premises underlying the roles and expectations of women and men. But the aging of the population, and its implications for women as potential caregivers to the nation, has not received enough attention from feminist or traditional women's organizations.

Probably most of us prefer to put off consideration of our own aging and the end of life as long as possible. Yet this is as profound a woman's issue as equal pay for comparable work, or violence against women, or any of the equity issues that have come to the fore in the last decade. There are no easy answers. To what extent are women ready to give up their work, their societal concerns, and their social existence beyond the confines of the household? Caregiving is an act of love—with consequences.

In every crisis lies the potential for a new start. In the long-term health care crisis, those who are most affected can take the lead in pointing out new directions and halting outdated practices. The positive side of the crisis is the potential that women represent for altering this nation's long-term care policies. If and when consciousness is sufficiently raised, women's organizations could force policy makers to consider alternatives. Alternatives that avoid exploitation of women will undoubtedly be more costly, but they will be more in line with the nation's professed concern for the welfare of the aged.

Women, Take Care

Recognizing that the caregiver must step out onto center stage, the OWL National Task Force on Caregivers began research on this book. The Task Force includes OWL activists, professionals who assist caregivers, attorneys, and caregivers themselves. We began a three-year process of research into the demographics that mean more and more women will face a period of caregiving in their lives; into the medical care system that prolongs life while doing little for those who spend their last years in chronic illness; into the economics of caregiving, which often push middle-class wives into poverty; and into the laws that can make caregiving more difficult, complicated, and financially disastrous than it need be.

The Task Force members interviewed hundreds of women

who were caring for husbands, fathers, mothers, and other relatives. We spoke with women who were caring for a relative all alone, at home, 24 hours a day, and with women who were juggling paid employment and caregiving. We spoke with women who had the (still exceptional) help of excellent support services in their communities and with women who got no help at all and had even been virtually abandoned by their doctors. We spoke with women whose families made their tasks lighter, women whose families harassed or ignored them, and women whose only family member was the relative they cared for. We spoke with women who chose caregiving gladly as a final act of great love, with women who felt trapped by caregiving being forced on them, and with women whose feelings were mixed. From many parts of the United States, women who learned of the project wrote down their experiences and added their letters to the growing articulation of the caregiver's voice.

Then, as the Task Force was completing the first stage of writing this book, two of the principal authors, Tish Sommers and Laurie Shields, suddenly experienced the issue in a highly personal way. Tish had survived cancer two decades earlier; now it recurred, and Laurie became her primary caregiver in the final months of her life. For the previous fifteen years, Tish had been the leading activist in the country for older women's issues. She gave "displaced homemakers" their name, and co-founded with Laurie a national movement that led to passage of a federal law funding local centers to give education and vocational training. The two also co-founded and led the Older Women's League.

When her cancer recurred, Tish remained a committed organizer and agitator for OWL through her very last days. She used what she called "deathbed power" to persuade funders to donate to OWL projects that she was determined would outlive her. She made a checklist of tasks, and completed them all before she consented to take the painkillers that brought relief, but dulled her mind. Tasks she could not finish she entrusted to others.

One of her final projects was this book. She and Laurie found that as they went through the actual experience of caregiving, their understanding of the issue changed and deepened. The insights of those final months are, we hope, reflected throughout the book. In the last chapter, Laurie and Tish have told their own stories, in Tish's words: "sharing the dying experience, not with avoidance and sorrow, but with joy and a great deal of love." Tish's dictation of her part was one of the last things she did before her death.

The result of this process, we hope, is a book that presents the complexities of the problem in such a way that they don't mask the human anguish that lies beneath the surface. If you are a caregiver or know you will eventually be one, this book will be a support group in written form. Like the group Clemmie Barry founded, *Women Take Care* will provide you with useful information and relief in the sharing of the stories of others. If you work as a professional with caregivers, this book will give you a new perspective. But above all, this book is addressed to you if you are not now a caregiver and have never considered the possibility, because you, like most women, probably will become a caregiver at some point in your life, and may find yourself unprepared for a task that society is making unnecessarily difficult.

This is a book for *all* women and men who care about women. Our underlying purpose in writing it is to raise consciousness on an invisible issue that will affect most of us profoundly, so that we can look forward more clearly toward our own futures, to better sort out guilt from public pressure, and take part in the public debate which is in the making. When large numbers of women embrace this issue, it will have significant impact on the realities of growing old. *Women Take Care* is both a statement of fact and a warning.

1

Who Are the Caregivers?

Contrary to prevalent myths, 95 percent of elderly people do not live in nursing homes. Even if they are disabled enough to need the kind of care provided in institutions, the majority live outside of them, in their communities. In 1985, 1.4 million people over 65 lived in nursing homes. But another 5.2 million people who were disabled enough to need help with day-to-day tasks such as food preparation, dressing, and bathing lived alone or with family. Each of these numbers is expected to double by the year 2000.

Some disabled older people who live outside of nursing homes hire paid caregivers, others receive services funded by the government or sponsored by churches or charities. But most of them (80 to 90 percent) are cared for by families. In about three-fourths of the cases, the caregiver is a woman.

Most often the caregivers are older women, who themselves are likelier than their younger counterparts to have health problems. The average age of a wife who cares for her husband is 65, and 30 percent are over age 74. The majority of daughters giving care are over 50. Because it is the oldest people who are most likely to be severely disabled, the oldest subgroups of both wives and daughters often have the most disabled relatives to care for.

The financial and health status of many caregivers is precarious. About one-third are poor; close to half are in fair or poor health. The amount of care they provide is staggering. For 30 to 40 percent of caregivers, their work over and above their normal household duties or paid employment is equivalent to a full-time job. In many cases, the job goes on 24 hours a day. All of this adds up to millions of women giving billions of hours of care every year.

These numbers give a sense of the vast amount of care that women are providing, unpaid, in the home. But numbers tell only part of the story. They don't tell what caregiving is like, whether the women have chosen this role or had it thrust upon them, how it affects the rest of their lives. To get that part of the story, we interviewed over two hundred caregivers who spoke openly about their caregiving experiences. There is no "typical" caregiver. But the four stories* we present here show some of the major themes that recurred in these women's lives.

"I Want You As Long As You Want to Stay"

Alice, when asked why she was the caregiver, responded, "I imagine every woman who becomes a caregiver did the same as I did . . . her husband got sick and she had no choice."

When it was pointed out that her husband could have gone to a convalescent home, she admitted even the doctors had recommended that. But she added, "I felt that whatever happened, I wanted to have him at home. I think they thought it was too big a job. He is totally paralyzed and I'm not too young and not trained in this field. The doctors told us he probably wouldn't

---

*Throughout this book, pseudonyms are used except when the stories are by members of the OWL Caregiver Task Force.

live but I thought that if that was true, the last part of his life would be richer at home than in a hospital or a convalescent home. But also, in my own mind I thought I knew Art pretty well. I thought he could go on for several years. Whichever way it went, I just thought he should be home."

Despite Alice's initial comment indicating she had "no choice," she did choose positively—lovingly and willingly—to care for Art. The focal point of that care was whatever was needed for his comfort and convenience.

> I just pushed all the furniture back and made room for a wheelchair. We had a neighbor build these wooden frames in the hallway against the wall where his wheelchair bumps into it. And we put the same little narrow guards around the furniture so he can bang into it all he wants. We gave away the big TV that used to be there and got rid of all the stuff that had been part of our decorating scheme for the living room. Our neighbor built a table high enough so Art can get up close in the wheelchair. And he built a little file cabinet for Art's personal papers. Art has a little TV and all his music tapes; he's got his shortwave, his cordless phone, police scanner and everything he enjoys. I put up a lot of his plaques and things that were on the wall downstairs where his office was. Of course, he'll never get downstairs again, and it would be a crime to deny him anything just for the sake of orderliness in the house. That isn't important and one hundred years from now it won't make any difference.

Alice and Art also dealt with Art's problems together. The first and biggest hurdle was accepting the fact that his paralysis was an accident. In the process of having radiation for a small tumor, his spinal cord was hit.

At the very first I cried and swore and prayed, equally, for about three months. Art and I talked about what the horrible mistake would cost him. We got mad as hell. It's just unbelievable that this could have happened to him. But then we realized there was no going back and we couldn't permit ourselves to get bitter and hateful, even when there's been such a horrendous error, because if you dwell on your hatred, it's awfully hard to move ahead.

They also discussed both the short-range and long-range plans, including figuring out what Art would do if Alice died first.

Art is totally dependent on me. If anything happened to me he wouldn't die, but he would be in terrible shape. We talk about it a lot. And we both have had new wills made. I have insurance for convalescent hospitalization for him and for me. And we have talked about what he should do. Talking these things out helps you have a pattern, and I think it's important that people like Art have some sense of security that planning ahead offers.

Strong support systems are absolutely essential in a caregiver's life. Alice had connections through her church to obtain the services of young seminarians. Their help freed her for part of the day, even though it wasn't the best of all situations.

From the beginning, real on-the-spot help came from the church. The women got together—even signed up—and would come in here. I don't think I cooked a meal for probably three months. And the men came and did chores around the place and helped in the house when they could. It was terrific. It wasn't just that they brought things, it

24

was the fact that they were here in the house with me and let me talk, although I have no idea what I said. But it was such a relief.

Both Art and Alice were then in their late 70s. Alice had a heart condition for twenty-five years, which called for her carrying nitroglycerin. This was a determining factor in their decision to hire help, even though it was minimal: five and a half hours a day, roughly 8:30 A.M. to 2:00 P.M. From 2:00 P.M. throughout the night, Alice was the primary caregiver.

I've learned to do many things. I'm not trying to be a nurse but I am alone with him in the night. Learning about bladder care and giving pills is simple. But the first thing is, you're not only his friend, you're his closest friend. You are the one who stands there in the middle of the night when he doesn't think he will live 'til morning. And somehow you both make it through. We know every day what our problem is. And I say to him every morning, we'll make it a good day. At night he'll tell me sometimes, "It's been a real good day."

Asked what she'd learned or gained from her experience as a caregiver, Alice answered:

Well, I suppose if you are going to talk about yourself you talk about spiritual self, and of course, you can't go through something like this without deepening the Christ of your own being— your own spiritual self. So the spiritual self has certainly been enriched.

And I think you do learn to be more appreciative of people

when they come to help you and see you. You see someone
go through what Art has gone through with the grace,
dignity, decency, and effort—God! The effort that man
puts out! Sometimes when I talk to him in the night, I'll
say, "Well, you know I want you as long as you want to
stay and I'll take care of you, but I know that when you've
had enough, you'll go." And then I always try to tell him
how much I love him, and I always tell him how much he's
done for other people. I want him to go out realizing that
his life has been of value to many people. I think you learn
way down below the surface of yourself and your mate.
It's an experience that I think is enriching. I don't wish it
on everybody and I didn't ask for it, but I can't think of
any way that my own life and my usefulness could have
been enhanced any more than this.

Almost three years after Alice brought Art home, she had to
place him in a nursing home for two weeks while she had ex-
ploratory surgery. She was diagnosed as having cancer of the
pancreas. Afterwards, she brought Art home again, where he
died, three months later. By this time, Alice was 80 years old,
and her son wanted her to move to another state with him. But
she opted to stay on alone in her home. She started chemo-
therapy, and members of her church set up a regular schedule of
visits to check up on her.

A Mother and Daughter

Dolores and Dorothy are a mother and daughter who cared for
Dolores' husband (Dorothy's father) when he had terminal cancer.
First, Dolores' story:

My husband died at 75 of cancer, after a long and debilitating illness. It started as a prostate cancer, which surgery

held in suspension for a few years, but it eventually developed into a widespread malignant invasion of his entire body. This process was spread over a period of eleven years, during which he had ups and downs. Gradually he turned into a bedridden invalid, totally dependent on me for his daily care.

The last three years were the most demanding. I was 71 when he died. The last year was devastating; it became a 24-hour job and I got little sleep because of his extreme restlessness. The last few months of his life he was given Dilaudin, a morphine derivative, that caused him to have hallucinations. His sleeplessness caused my sleeplessness because he constantly called to me in his drug-laden state.

My lack of sleep made deep inroads on my sense of reality. I have several gaps in my memory of that terrible time, probably because I was carrying on as I have been programmed to do, operating at full speed with vastly reduced amounts of energy. I doubt if I would have been able to last if my daughter hadn't been able to stay with us and help care for her father the last two months. What happened, however, is that there were now two of us who were going without sleep, as my home is small and not soundproof. There was no escape from that constant and pathetic calling, "Honey. Honey. Honey, come and get me out of here."

I decided that he should die at home for several reasons. After his last short stay in the hospital, they said they had done all they could for him. The alternative of a nursing home seemed so unkind. It would have almost seemed inhuman. Even if I had been able to do it financially (which I was not), I would not have been able emotionally to let him die there alone. The care at nursing homes, while very expensive, is also uneven and unreliable. In some instances there is outright neglect. I could not do this to my husband.

Throughout a long marriage, he had earned my love and respect. As long as I was still on my feet, I wanted to help him die.

I experienced emotional problems because I was coping with an unforeseen domestic crisis with a bare minimum of tools with which to solve it. Anxiety loomed large. At the last, the cancer destroyed the 7th nerve in his head, causing one eye to remain permanently open (it had to be bandaged shut). It also caused a malfunction of his jaw. He could not chew and could not wear his dentures. All his food had to be put through a blender so he had only to swallow it. As he got weaker, it became increasingly hard to get enough food down as I fed him. I became so afraid he was going to starve to death that on the few occasions when I could fall asleep, my sleep would turn into a nightmare that my husband was dying of starvation and I was to blame. I was never free of this free-floating anxiety.

Isolation was an important part of this stressful time. While I have what I consider good neighbors, I live in a rural area, and houses are not close. My neighbors are not the kind of people who "run in" as legends tell us rural people do. These people are all retired from large cities, where people tend to stay to themselves. They responded well when I asked, but I have a personal problem about asking for help. I have been socialized to remain independent as long as possible and this training does get in my way in a time of crisis.

The outstanding memory I have is of being abandoned by the institutions I formerly had a great deal of respect for. The last thing I remember of the hospital was being told they needed his bed and I was to take him out of there. No advice as to what I was to do with him, just take him away. By this time, I was beginning to suspect he was dying, although no one ever said as much to me.

I got no information from his doctor or the nurse in his office. I inadvertently heard of the Visiting Nurses Association from the alternate doctor in the office. The VNA saved what was left of my sanity by giving me information, as well as help three days a week. I was reassured that I was "doing it right." Also, they told me about *hospice*, which helped to give me (and eventually my daughter) occasional short respite times.

However, by the time I received this help, I was seriously near the breaking point myself. I had eye surgery just after my daughter came to help. My recovery has been very slow. My age has something to do with it, of course, but the emotional hurts of feeling lost and abandoned by society are not easily healed.

Like many caregivers, Dolores cared for her husband for a long time, and the demands on her accelerated as his condition worsened. Her story also illustrates some other common facets of the caregiving situation. She got little help or useful information from medical professionals, not even the information that her husband was dying. She was left to find services that could help on an almost random basis of luck.

She chose to provide care right up until the day of her husband's death, not wanting him to have to go to a nursing home. While there are good quality nursing homes, they are rare and, as Dolores notes, expensive. Many caregivers view them as the last possible resort; couples make pacts to avoid them. Many very stressed caregivers, like Dolores, simply refuse to consider the option.

Dolores' daughter, Dorothy, helped with her father's care for a much shorter period. Because her time as a caregiver was unexpected, she saw things much more sharply than did her mother. The experience was so deeply felt that five years later, as she told her story, she seemed to be reliving it. Dorothy's story:

In April of 1981, at the request of my parents, I returned from Berlin, West Germany (where I was living with my husband and child) to help my parents during my mother's eye surgery, which she had needed for some time. I had planned to stay two weeks, until my mother was recovered enough to continue her long-term care of my father. I ended up staying two and a half months, until my father died.

My mother's surgery went well, but my father's cancer got progressively worse day by day, right before my eyes. He was still eating well—though all the food had to be pureed—but he lost weight. He was, however, still able to get around by himself: to the bathroom, to the dinner table, and, occasionally, out on the beautiful deck surrounding their small home. Then, about three weeks after mother's surgery, his cancer began to spread fast throughout his body, causing him to become bedridden.

When I first came, I became the caregiver for them both, with no respite. The emotional atmosphere of having two patients whom I loved very much, combined with the magnetic pull of my family back in Europe, was almost unbearable. The inconvenience was great for me. My parents and I discussed it many times, always coming up with the same answer: their need was greater than my inconvenience.

My husband and our son, who was 17 years old, were left on their own in Germany during this desperate time in our lives. Our two daughters lived here in the states. One, 22, lived and worked in Sacramento, and the other, 19, was enrolled at San Francisco State University. It was a very stressful experience for all of us. As a family, we had always been close, no matter where we lived. Thank heaven for the telephone! We talked often, but the separation was traumatic. My parents lived in Penn Valley, California, so all calls were long distance.

It was a time full of anxiety and guilt, mostly due to our inexperience. I was not prepared for the dying process, for our society does not teach us to die, only to be born and to be young and beautiful. It was appalling to watch the wasting of my father's body.

At first, he was up several times each night, shuffling down the hall to the bathroom across from my bedroom, tapping his cane on the floor, disturbing my rest. Then, as the disease caused even more disintegration, he needed help getting to the bathroom and mother and I divided up the nights we were "on duty." Soon, he needed constant care and became bedridden, with a toilet beside his bed. The closeness of the situation, and the sudden need to be more than a daughter, stretched our relationship. Where was our God? I still remember the guilt. More than once I wished my father would die. A couple of times I even said so, out loud to my mother. I needed periodic *overnight* respite from this constant stress. So did my mother. My father was very concerned for my welfare, as I was for theirs. However, there was no such overnight relief.

For four weeks I had two patients, 24 hours a day. My father's right eye had been destroyed and my mother had had eye surgery. I was dressing an eye on each three times a day as well as the general strenuous care for the terminal patient. In retrospect, I wonder how I survived. I am not a nurse, merely a human being with no choice in what was happening to me.

My brothers apparently thought they had a choice, for they only dealt with it all by long distance. One brother even took his girlfriend on a two-week vacation on the day my mother got out of the hospital from eye surgery, leaving me alone with two patients. He had no steady job and hadn't for some time. He could have been of tremendous help to us. My brothers were very fearful of the death process. I was, too. However, I could not ignore it.

My oldest brother called long distance and accused me of keeping our father out of the hospital. When I told him that the hospital had released Daddy because they needed the bed for someone they could help, my brother merely scoffed. I told him that the best way to find out about the condition of his father, and the way in which he was being care for, was to come up to Penn Valley and observe. I would also be glad to have the help and moral support. He said he couldn't manage that, and that I ought to know better than to suggest such a thing, for after all, he had job commitments.

My older daughter would come up from Sacramento on weekends, when she could, to help with the cleaning and shopping. One weekend when I was really on the ragged edge and needed moral support, she called and said she "needed some time off." I very tersely asked her, "When do I get time off?" This resulted in her hiring a night nurse on two separate occasions so that Mother and I could get some much-needed rest. However, because of the thin walls in the house, we were still kept awake as Daddy talked with the nurse. He was constantly telling the nurse how to care for him, or was calling out "Honey" for my mother to show the nurse exactly what to do. It was a nightmare.

My other daughter was away from home for the first time. She was not able to come and help becaue of her school demands. Taking advantage of the habit of usually having my attention, she called one day to cry on my shoulder about breaking up with her boyfriend, only to have me say, "Don't bother me with your problems." I had suddenly become unavailable to her and to the rest of my family.

I went along with my mother's decision to keep my father at home until he died. But we made this decision at our own risk. My father's doctor was a real downer, as was his nurse. And, once checked out of the hospital, we received no additional help or information from hospital personnel or my father's doctor, his nurse, or office staff.

We were just lucky the day my mother stumbled on an informed person, Daddy's doctor's alternate. He told my mother, by telephone, of the Visiting Nurses Association, and they in turn told us of the Thrift Shop Cancer Aid Society of Grass Valley and, eventually, hospice. Except for these organizations, we were isolated.

Few of the neighborhood women came to visit us. When I asked neighborhood men to help keep cars running and the outside yard from going completely to seed, they were very guarded, but they were willing to help when contacted.

My father didn't want hospice around because he thought they were a religious group. We had them anyway at the very end, out of desperation. There was no one else to turn to for aid. As to counseling and education of the sick and dying, the information is there only if you know where to look. The Visiting Nurses Association was a blessing. They were convinced that my father was better off at home and was getting better care than in a convalescent home.

I had to educate myself about in-dwelling catheters so I could get past the doctor's nurse and convince the doctor that my father needed one (or rather, that I needed fewer wet bedclothes). The Visiting Nurses finally stepped in and called the doctor's office and we got the in-dwelling catheter. I wanted my parents to change doctors, but that was unthinkable to them, although they were not impressed with their doctor either. I discovered that debilitating diseases such as cancer can cause one to grow inward for protection.

Anything or anyone new results in emotional trauma that one so ill hasn't the energy to deal with.

Every morning the last two or three weeks of Daddy's life, Mother and I would take our morning tea out on the sunny deck and discuss our situation. It always began with our feelings of inadequacy in caring for Daddy. We really were inexperienced, though we both had researched the disease so we could describe to the doctor what we felt we needed in caring for Daddy. We also discussed putting him in a "home" for the final weeks. This was only because we felt so helpless and exhausted. We both wondered how much longer we could go on keeping our head and our physical health, caring for him night and day with no respite.

My father talked all night, re-living his childhood, my childhood, and my children's childhood. He would sing vaudeville songs to me and tell bawdy jokes, a side of my father I had never witnessed. He was restless and awake most of the 24 hours. If he did sleep, he would awaken within an hour and begin talking again. It was as though a camera in his head had been speeded up, making him run instead of walk through life's memories and experiences.

One night very late, I had just fallen asleep and Daddy called to me to come help him to the toilet beside his bed. I wearily made my way down the hall. He was sitting on the side of the high hospital bed, very apologetic as usual. I assured him it was no problem and reached up and put my arms around him to help him lift himself off the bed, and position him to sit on the toilet. His knees just wouldn't hold him up, and I remember absolute fright that if I dropped him, he'd most likely break a bone or something equally as dangerous. We sort of both fell onto the toilet.

I developed a chronic back problem due to lifting and assisting my father in and out of bed and on and off the toilet. The countless household chores went on and on, keeping food not only in the larder but on the table, and keeping the garden outside from going to seed, which meant moving the hose and mowing the lawn once in a while.

Mostly, the outside work became a refuge from the dying process inside. My hands began to smell like my father's bowel movements. I just couldn't get the smell out no matter how or what I washed them with. It seems it never failed that the minute I sat down to a meal, he'd call and need to be cleaned up. The outside smelled so good. My eating habits also changed drastically, causing me to gain weight as never before. The less my father could eat, the more I ate. I lived with interrupted sleep and nightmares for several months after my father died. I still get tearful as I write this story. The frustration of trying desperately to help my parents, and to field the obstacles that were constantly being thrown from every conceivable direction, is still very vivid.

In looking back, I can't help but compare the birth of a newborn and the care it requires with the care of a terminal patient. They are both very dependent on their mother/ caregiver. Observe the networking that goes on when a newborn makes an entrance into our world. I was always surrounded with help and information when my babies were born. Comparing notes with other new mothers about a green bowel movement being the norm for a newborn was information gladly shared. On the other hand, the subjects of the bedridden cancer patient and the probable death are subjects that are avoided, even ignored. There is a definite need for information in dealing with death, no matter what the loved one's age. Death and dying are taboo subjects. No one wanted to talk to Mother and me, though we needed to talk about it.

All the stress, strain, emotional trauma, the never-ending

household chores, the new nursing chores I learned as we
went along in his new life "adventure," the separation from
my husband and son by an ocean, the terrible gulf that developed between me and my brothers (which hurts to this
day), the wonderful discovery that both of my daughters
could rise to a difficult situation and let me lean on them a
little, all this I would not have experienced had we put Daddy in a convalescent home. This, of course, I see in retrospect, but nonetheless, it is not lost on my soul and intellect.

The attitude of Dorothy's brothers is not unusual. Our society
persists in seeing males as providers and females as nurturers.
Dorothy traveled from another continent to be a caregiver; her
brothers would not cross part of a state, even though one was
unemployed. Daughters and daughers-in-law often face a choice
between their paid employment and caregiving or (as Dorothy
did) between their husbands/children and caregiving. Men rarely
are forced to confront such a choice.

Both Dorothy's and Dolores' health suffered, a common
problem we discuss more fully in Chapter 2. Both Dorothy and
Dolores felt the two needs that are probably most common among
caregivers: first, better information about the patient's illness and
guidance about giving care, and second, badly needed respite—
actual help to replace some of their efforts.

"I'm Not a Nurturing Person"

Not every woman is prepared to accept society's decree that
wives should take care of their ailing husbands. Jill openly
expressed her opposition to the role. "I don't want to be the
primary caregiver, because I can't be . . . I mean, it 's not part of
my makeup. I am not a nurturing person in the strictest sense of
the word. And I don't feel badly about that, it's just my nature.
I was never that way with my children, either."

But neither did she want her husband placed in an institutional setting. Ben, who suffered from Parkinson's, could be more comfortable in the familiar surroundings of their home. But the decision was not made without pain for Jill, given her honest assessment of her own nature.

You get to the point where you can continue doing for somebody what should be done, but you have to figure out whether you can handle it for yourself. I keep thinking that there is still life out there for me at the age of 65. I say, well, how much longer do I have? There's a lot of things I want to do with my life, and I feel like I'm giving up opportunities and it's the unfairness of it. Ben even understands that, and when he was much better he used to say so all the time. He said he didn't want me cheated out of living. Now he doesn't say that anymore because his need is greater.

He clings much more and that's the thing I can't handle. I feel smothered when he does it. Yet I understand his need, but that doesn't help me even if I understand it. Because I have needs, too. I think that is one of the things people need to understand about caregivers.

There should be some kind of "bill of rights" for caregivers spelling out that you can only give what you can give. And that should be acceptable. You shouldn't be criticized if you can't do more. And this bill of rights should include things you have to do for yourself. You have to be a caregiver for yourself, also. Unfortunately, in marriage, a woman ends up being a caregiver meeting her husband's needs. But there is nobody meeting her needs.

Despite her feelings, Jill was the primary caregiver for Ben, whose condition worsened when, in addition to Parkinson's, he developed Alzheimer's disease. She had outside help from time to time, but when Ben went to the hospital on one occasion, the doctor told her it was time to explore another alternative for his care. He also told her to think about her own health, which was deteriorating under the emotional and physical stress of dealing with Ben on a 24-hour basis.

> I guess I was waiting for him to say that. I was pleased he did because it released something in me. I didn't *have* to have the total responsibility of doing something with Ben. And that just opened all kinds of doors for me.

Suddenly the seven-room house that had been their home became an asset in providing alternatives to Jill's role as primary caregiver. One of the outside helpers she had used in the past, who had even stayed with Ben when she had to go out-of-town, was looking for a larger place for herself and her husband. Jill asked the helper to take care of Ben for a six-month trial, with the couple moving into the house and Jill getting a small apartment nearby.

> That was not an easy decision to make. It was a very painful thing and it took me a long time to think about leaving my home. But when I thought about the alternatives, of what I went through emotionally, it was not hard. This was an experiment for six months and the beauty of it was that I still had access to my home since I took care of Ben two days a week.

Living alone gave Jill a perspective on her own mortality. It helped soften the resentment she felt at enforced caregiving and the limits on her opportunities to be and to do.

> Death isn't as frightening as when I first began thinking about it. It's a normal process and if I haven't come to terms with it totally, I'm on my way. Because, actually, I've done most of the things I set out to do. I've had a very, very active full life and while I may have missed out on this or that, I really feel I've done most of the things I wanted to do.

The experiment ended before the six months were over because the young couple felt they needed more privacy than taking care of Ben allowed. Jill moved back and took over until Ben's death. But the time on her own, brief as it was, renewed her strength and courage. Most of all it helped her come to terms with living and dying.

No research has been done to tell us how many women, like Alice, gladly accept their role as caregiver and how many, like Jill, would choose otherwise if there were viable options. The caregivers we interviewed generally had a mixture of feelings, but guilt was prominent for most. We can surmise that strong social pressure causes a lot of this guilt. That, combined with the generally shared (but not always correct) view that nursing home care is a horrible alternative, and the high cost of nursing homes, probably means that many caregivers feel trapped. They'd rather not take on the role, but they see no way out. Some, like Jill, can work out a satisfactory solution. Most of the others cope as best they can. When a caregiver just can't cope, the result is sometimes elder abuse, as described in Chapter 6.

Caregivers in America today number in the millions. They

are drawn from every economic stratum, every ethnic group. There are probably as many stories, and as many unique configurations of problems, as there are caregivers. In the following chapter, we explore some of the more common emotional and physical problems caregivers face.

2

A Heavy Load: The Emotional and Physical Cost of Caregiving

"When someone calls me on the phone, and I've been by myself all day with Ben . . . I feel like a dam is breaking. You know, I can almost hear myself sputtering . . . tttttt. And that's not me, that's not part of my personality. I've got to communicate some way with somebody. And if I don't have it here with Ben . . . I've got to do it someplace. Otherwise, I'm not alive. That was the basis of our relationship: Ben and I had a highly intellectual relationship with each other, a challenging one. It's what I miss most."

—Jill

"I did the best I could for Dad. And I'm proud I did it. If I had it to do over again, which I may have to do with my husband's family, I would. When you are a caregiver, you are probably doing the most noble thing you could possibly do for somebody who really needs the help."

—Carol

"I think I do amazingly well for him. I try in every possible way to see that he is in as good a situation as I can put him in. But

41

because I'm not emotionally involved, I have a guilt feeling. I am
probably not as compassionate as I might be."

—Paula

"I have to watch every move that man makes. What if he gets a
spell and is just lying in the streets, like the police found him that
time? The minute I don't see him around the house, or he's not in
bed, then I start looking for him."

—Louise

Caregiving can be emotionally overwhelming. When a husband
or parent becomes dependent, whether gradually or suddenly, the
relationship with wife or daughter inevitably changes. The caregiver has many new worries: Is her relative in pain? Is she doing
enough? Are her finances going to survive this? Can she handle
the physical aspects of caregiving? How can she find out what to
do about problems like bladder control? One survey reported that
over half of female caregivers find their task emotionally difficult.

Often, caregivers face these problems alone. Overworked and
under stress, they experience a complicated mixture of emotions. The feelings can cover a wide range. Grief, loneliness,
frustration, anger, guilt, anxiety, and depression may all be
tangled up with love, pride, and a sense of personal accomplishment and strength.

"I Try to Be Tender, but It's Not a Husband and Wife Feeling"

Jill (whose story of caring for her husband, Ben, through Parkinson's and Alzheimer's disease is told in Chapter 1) mourned
because so much of the man she married was gone.

A husband and wife relationship to me is a partnership, and
once you become a caregiver, that's wrong. I no longer feel
myself a wife and I don't think of Ben as my husband. I

42

think of myself closer to being his mother. And when you start feeling those kinds of feelings toward your husband, why your whole approach to the relationship changes. I try to be tender, but it's not a husband and wife feeling for me.

Like Jill, many caregivers experience grief. They grieve for their lost relationship with a husband/parent, for their loss of identity as a functioning couple. But this is a different grief than grief at death. Loss through death is final. Most of the time, for the widow as for adult child, death brings closure. The loss most caregivers experience is open-ended; it can go on and on. They watch as a husband or parent gradually deteriorates, feeling helpless that they can't stop the process.

With Ben's illness, Jill lost the intellectual challenge of their relationship, which had included a lot of debate and discussion.

That intellectual stimulation was a really great thing. When that went, I could see everything going, going, going. I tried to bring it back in so many ways, but the doctor said it wasn't going to happen. And I kept denying it all the time.

For Jill, the grief was softened by what remained of the Ben she loved: "He's still kind and gentle. Around the house are many things he gave me and he gave me joy in so many ways," she said.

Caregivers also grieve for their lost lifestyles. Jill felt trapped at home with Ben 24 hours a day, felt she was being cheated out of life. And she also missed her social life.

I haven't been able to handle having our old friends come here, because we are both objects of pity. I can't handle that. I really don't want their pity. And Ben doesn't want it either. It's very awkward. People who knew Ben before stumble;

they make conversation with him and he can't respond. He just sits there and knows he can't say what he wants to.

Because loss of mental function was Ben's major problem, Jill felt lonely when she was with him. "Just because there's a body in the house doesn't mean it's not lonely. In fact, it's lonelier to have somebody in the next room you can't communicate with." Jill's loneliness was compounded by her feelings about her old friends.

Loneliness is often a by-product of the role for caregivers like Jill. But for others, loneliness may be caused by just being too busy and exhausted to keep up social contacts, or by being confined to the house 24 hours a day. In one survey, over half the women caring for an older relative said that it limited their social life. Loneliness due to isolation can have a profound and debilitating effect on the caregiver.

Caring for a parent, while often not as isolating as caring for a husband, can still be lonely. One woman spoke of no longer having enough time with her husband and children after she became her mother's full-time caregiver, even though they all lived in the same house. Another woman, retired and single, moved her mother into her own home. The mother was demanding, and the daughter organized her social life around activities her mother enjoyed, giving up her own friends and interests.

Anger is another common emotion among caregivers. Sometimes the anger is for family or friends who don't do enough. Dorothy, whose story is told in Chapter 1, was very angry at her brothers for not helping in the care of her father.

Caregivers also feel a sense of betrayal at systems they believed would support them. One woman spoke of being furious when she learned that Medicare would not pay for either nursing home or at-home care for her husband. She felt cheated by the system. She and her husband had saved hard for their retirement, but the savings would all have to be used to pay for nursing home care before she would receive any help.

Another frequently justified target of caregiver anger is the medical community, which fails to provide adequate information and assistance. Dorothy and Dolores found it almost impossible to get information from their doctor, even though they had read about the disease so they would know what questions to ask.

Often, too, the anger is turned on the disabled relative. Jill sometimes got mad at Ben for being at his worst with her, and handling himself better with a paid attendant. She recounted an incident:

> He seemed to be more incontinent when I was around than when he was around other people. One morning, he said he had to go to the bathroom. I interpreted that to mean that he had to have a bowel movement. So I got him ready to go into the bathroom and he stood there with a urinal two feet away from him and just urinated all over the floor. I really got mad and I yelled at him.

And on the heels of her anger, Jill always felt the occupational hazard of caregiving: *guilt.* She struggled with guilt over not being a more nurturing person, feeling sometimes that the part-time attendant she hired handled Ben better than she did.

Guilt is often the result of conflicting feelings. Jill's anger at Ben for incontinence was mixed with feelings of love and grief, making her feel guilty when she expressed the anger.

What to Do?

When the relationship has been strong, it can help a caregiver cope with her new feelings. "We had a good marriage," said Jill. "That's one of the things that made me continue, because Ben was a good man." When the relationship before the illness was not good, caregiving can be more difficult, as Paula's story (later in this chapter) illustrates.

Family and friends can also help. Support can make a big difference, whether it is direct help with caregiving, caring phone calls, or financial assistance. Organized community resources can also be important. Jill got help from two organizations in California: Marin Senior Day Services in Marin County and Family Survival Project in San Francisco. "I can tell you, if it wasn't for those two organizations, I don't think I could have handled it emotionally. I would have broken down," she said.

Many caregivers also find this is a time in their lives that puts relationships to an acid test; they find out which ones are really true ones. Said Jill:

> I found out who my real friends are. I found out that friendship is something very, very precious and that you really don't have a lot of friends. You have a lot of acquaintances, but you have few friends. And, I found out those I could confide in and those I chose not to because I recognized that we didn't have that basic relationship. But I did discover I had a friend in my son. I probably had that with him before, but it never occurred to me to look at him on that level. It was really a glorious experience. And it's brought our family closer together.
>
> Also, I've learned to ask my children to help me with things. That's a different role for me, because I've always been the doer. When I get so desperate sometimes and call them up and weep on their shoulders, I don't feel any kind of resistance from any of them. And when they ask me how I feel, I tell them. Not that they can do much about it, but telling is important.

The time of family crisis can also lead to psychological growth and enhanced freedom. Said Jill, while Ben was still alive:

46

I think I know myself better now. I know what I can do and what I can't do. It's strengthened my will to find my own way because I recognize what's happening is that I am waiting for my husband to die. And rather than wait until it happens, I'm trying to build my life before it happens.

"I'm Proud I Did It. It's Probably the Most Noble Thing One Could Possibly Do"

Carol's father lived on his own near her home. He had developed Alzheimer's disease, but covered up his symptoms for years. When he needed to go into a hospital for eye surgery, the doctors told Carol that her father's Alzheimer's had progressed to a point where he could no longer live on his own. Carol put him in a convalescent home. "He was okay there, but he wasn't real happy. And of course, I loved my dad very much, and kept running up there, worrying about how he was being cared for, and it dawned on me: why was I leaving Dad there, when I could do the same thing in my own home? He'd be a lot happier."

It was sad for Carol to watch her father deteriorate. "Daddy had always been a brilliant man. And when he reached the level of a 6-year-old child, that hurt," she said. "I had to treat him as a mother speaking to a child. And that's difficult to cope with."

Carol also felt frustration, a common feeling among caregivers. Her father would accuse Carol and her husband and sons of stealing things. "He'd get so upset about somebody stealing something when it hadn't been stolen. And you just couldn't point it out to him. It got terribly frustrating."

Taking care of a disabled parent or husband can also create anxiety and fear, as the caregiver finds herself in a new and sensitive situation she doesn't know how to manage. Carol became very anxious about her father's sexuality.

Sometimes he'd get confused and think I wasn't his daughter.

47

He'd think I was his wife. He'd think I should go to bed with him rather than sleep with my husband. We had jealousy problems. I was embarrassed and upset and didn't always know how to handle it.

Compounding these feelings was a lack of sleep.

It was definitely 24-hour caregiving. He'd wake up at three o'clock every morning, thinking it was time to get up. He'd holler and get us all up and we'd have to talk to him and explain that it was dark outside and he had to go back to bed and go to sleep.

Young mothers are often tired for the first few months after a baby is born because they have responsibility around the clock, including getting up several times a night for feedings. Eventually, though, the baby sleeps through the night. For someone caring for an adult, however, round-the-clock responsibility can go on indefinitely, and interrupted sleep can last for years. And the relative gets steadily worse, the reverse of a baby's progress. It's no wonder that caregiving can cause such deterioration.

Even when their relative sleeps through the night, the caregiver's anxiety and stress can lead to insomnia. Whatever the source, constant fatigue can lower a caregiver's resistance to disease and affect her mental health.

Carol joined a local support group for caregivers. "It was very helpful. It gave me a chance to vent my frustration and I got a lot of good feedback that helped me cope with what I was up against. I realized I wasn't alone, that there were other people who had the same problems." The group, plus her supportive family, helped stem the "hopeless, helpless" feelings she had almost all of the time. Another support was being able to take her father to an adult day care center for 5 hours a day, although "a little longer would have helped more," she said.

The complicated emotions of caregiving go on after the person being cared for dies. Carol found it took a long time to put her life back together.

> I was exhausted just from having to take care of him so long. And after he died, there was a lot to deal with. If you don't let the emotional feelings out, they just well up inside you and make you really ill. You have to give yourself some time.

Carol had to put her career as a real estate agent on hold while she cared for her father, but she has no regrets. She felt a sense of accomplishment that she'd done the best she could. And in spite of all the heartache, she says "it was a very worthwhile experience."

"I Have a Guilt Feeling. I'm Probably Not As Compassonate As I Should Be."

Due to the abnormal stress and burden they carry, it is probably normal for caregivers to be depressed. Most caregivers are never treated for clinical depression, yet many experience symptoms such as tearfulness, fatigue, sleep disturbance, or eating disorders. Ongoing depression places additional stress on the caregiver and depletes the personal resources she needs to manage her difficult role.

Paula's husband, Gene, suffered from Parkinson's disease for thirty years. For a long time he did not need care, but gradually he needed more and more. Paula took care of him single-handedly until a visiting nurse "instructed me in no uncertain terms that if I didn't acquire some help, he needed to go to a nursing home. He was falling and injuring himself. He had abrasions and bruises. He wasn't being bathed frequently enough because of the risk of falling, and he just didn't look well." Paula then hired an attendant 4 hours a day, which was all she could afford. Paula coped with all this by not feeling.

> I think I have some kind of emotional block that is protective. It keeps me from feeling despair. If I felt it all, I suppose I could cope, but I'd really be miserable. This has been my general pattern in life. It's not unique to this situation. Apparently, I'm surviving.

Unlike Jill, Paula did not have a strong prior relationship to fall back on. She felt an emotional distance from Gene, but she didn't think it was because of his illness. "It's been the pattern of our relationship. Not hostile, just detached." She felt guilty that she did not feel more emotionally involved with his care.

She frequently felt angry at Gene because it seemed to her that he was often more helpless than he needed to be. "Some of his weakness and indifference to his personal care seemed voluntary," she said. When the visiting nurse pointed out Paula's neglect, it compounded her guilt.

Many caregivers feel guilty about their dislike of the caregiving role. Paula believed she was not really a nurturer, but because she felt a sense of responsibility, she learned to do what was necessary. Still, she felt guilty about her lack of compassion.

Many caregivers have mixed feelings. They want their relative to live and improve if possible, but they also hope the relative can die peacefully and be released from misery. The conflict can make the caregiver feel guilty for thinking of death as a viable option.

Caregivers may also feel guilty about past problems in the relationship and try to make up for them in the new situation. As one woman said, "We used to fight all the time. I was always nagging him. I want to make it up to him now, so I take real good care of him and make sure he's got everything he needs."

Paula also felt very anxious about her paid attendant. She depended on his help, but he was an elderly man and she feared he, too, might become ill. "If he were unavailable, what's the alternative?" she asked. One day Gene got mad at the attendant and told him he was fired. The attendant left. Paula recalled, "I was in a panic. I was afraid he wouldn't come back."

She also had a fear common among many caregivers: that she would not survive caregiving financially. She couldn't afford to have Gene in a nursing home; it would leave her with no resources. She just kept hoping she could keep him at home and if he did finally have to go to a nursing home, the time would be brief. At the age of 68, she decided to go back to work so she could pay for more hours of attendant care.

The overall undefined and transitional status of the role of caregiver can be very frustrating, especially for a wife and especially if it goes on for a long, open-ended time. As Paula noted,

> It's almost widowhood without the title. It limits all sorts of pleasures. There are no activities you can engage in, no social life. You have to do everything independently, and yet you are not free to move independently. It has the worst aspects of being a wife and a widow.

"It's a Wonder I Don't Get Sick Myself"

At the time we interviewed her, Louise had cared for Harry through a series of strokes for seventeen years. Her only real breaks had been when he was hospitalized after the acute phase of a stroke. Harry was able to walk, but he had little control over his bowels and bladder.

> I have to be very careful when he messes the bed, which he

does quite often. I have to change his underwear twice a day. He doesn't get to the bathroom quite fast enough, so I change his bed again. I have to clean it all up. I'm always disinfecting and opening the windows. I don't have rugs in the bedroom. If he did that on rugs, there would be terrible stains. This way, I can scrub, and it's nice and clean again. I let the whole house go until I can take care of the bedroom for him. We have a lot of people come to visit us and I wouldn't want somebody to come into the room while he's sleeping and say, "Oh, my God, when did she clean his bedroom last."

Louise also had to change and wash Harry's clothes frequently because he got them dirty when he tried to eat. Harry had trouble communicating what he wanted, so Louise would try to do various things for him until she hit on the one he wanted. That was frustrating for her. Harry took out his own frustrations with his condition on their house. He kicked a hole in an outside wall and broke several dining room chairs by throwing them around. Harry occasionally wandered away from the house, and once the police found him lying in the street. Louise said she had to "watch every move that man makes."

Louise felt it was "a wonder I don't get sick myself." At her yearly physical, the family doctor marveled that she maintained good general health. Her only problem was an arthritic knee. Like many caregivers, Louise put off attending to this health problem because she didn't know who would care for Harry. "My knee is just terrible. If I sit down for too long, I have a heck of a time getting up. But once I'm up, I can keep walking. I should have an operation, but I've waited too long. I don't want to go to the hospital because I'd have to be there five days."

Louise was able to call on her son and daughter-in-law, who often brought dinner over for her and Harry. She also took Harry to an adult day care center for a few hours each day, which helped. But like most caregivers, she couldn't afford to hire household help to lighten the physical burden she was under.

Stress on the Body. The actual physical labor involved in caregiving places a great deal of stress on the body. Frequently, heavy lifting is part of the task, as it was for Dorothy and Dolores, whose stories are told in Chapter 1. A husband or parent may have to be helped in and out of bed, to the bath or the toilet. Bedding may need to be changed frequently and more than the usual amount of cleaning and laundry may be necessary, as it was for Louise.

All the extra work and lifting puts strain on the body, especially the knees, hips, and lower back. This can lead to bursitis, damage to the discs in the lower spine, and lower back pain. Elderly caregivers, especially women, may suffer from osteoarthritis, a joint disease common among the aged. Excessive strain on the joints can speed up degenerative changes that occur as a result of this disease. The pain of arthritis is often made worse by motion and weight-bearing. Younger caregivers who place repeated strain on their joints from heavy lifting may be predisposed to developing arthritis in their later years. Elderly women may have the additional problem of osteoporosis (thinning of the bones), which often causes back pain and an increased susceptibility to fractures.

Sources of Help. It is usually possible to find some help for heavy physical chores. Equipment that can help with lifting and heavy labor can be rented or ordered from catalogues (see "Resources"). For example, a hospital bed with a trapeze bar can allow a disabled person to lift him or herself out of bed.

Equipment doesn't always have to be complex or expensive. Many caregivers show ingenuity in developing ways to make their tasks easier and their relatives' lives more comfortable. In Chapter 10, Laurie Shields describes how the oxygen machine her husband needed kept him confined to the bedroom, until she came up with the idea of adding longer tubing. This simple addition allowed him to get up and move around the house.

A support group can be a good place to find solutions to the physical problems of caregiving. Other caregivers who are coping with the same problems often have a new slant or a new technique. One caregiver tells how a support group solved a problem:

> At one of our meetings, I was telling the women how difficult it was for me to give my husband a bath. I'd get him on the shower chair in the tub and use the hand-held spray, but I managed to flood the bathroom floor every time. One of the other wives asked if the shower chair had holes in it to drain the water. I said no, I'm using the one they gave me at the hospital. The woman told me I could get the other type of chair in town, and it's made all the difference in the world!

Some support groups also sponsor workshops that give practical information on caregiving.

Nurses, physical therapists, and occupational therapists can also be sources of advice. They can teach proper lifting techniques and advise as to what devices might be useful. National organizations have been formed to help families cope with particular diseases. They may also be good sources of information on the physical aspects of their particular disease. A list of these organizations appears in the "Resources" section of this book.

When Caregiving Is Life-Threatening

The emotional strain of caregiving, coupled with the sheer physical labor often involved, creates a high level of stress, which, in itself, is harmful to a person's health. Stress is a prime factor in the development of high blood pressure, stroke, and heart disease. It may have a link to cancer (this link is being explored). Any many health problems—among them allergies, migraine headaches, and digestive disorders such as ulcers and diverticulitis—are made worse by stress.

Stress triggers an inborn response in us known as the "fight-or-flight" reaction. When we are faced with situations that require us to adjust, our bodies automatically begin producing adrenalin. Adrenalin increases blood pressure, heart rate, rate of breathing, blood flow to the muscles, and metabolism. Under normal circumstances, this reaction is a protective mechanism, but when we are faced with repeated stressful events and when circumstances prevent us from fighting or escaping that stress (as is often the case for caregivers), the repeated activation of the fight-or-flight response has an adverse effect on the body.

Emergencies can also create stress. Long episodes of chronic illness are usually punctuated by crises of some kind. Depending on the nature of the disease, the crisis might be a fall, another stroke, a serious bowel difficulty, a violent emotional outburst, or even an infection like the flu that is compounded by disability. Crises can add a special kind of stress, creating more work and adding acute anxiety.

Stress can also lead to poor eating habits, which can show up as loss of appetite or overeating. In either case, it can result in poor nutrition.

The demands of caregiving can lead some caregivers to drug or alcohol abuse. If the caregiver is already taking several prescription drugs, she may not realize what is happening. In addition, the effect of many drugs can be intensified by the use of alcohol. When some blood pressure medications interact with alcohol, for example, they cause fainting. Heavy drinking or drug abuse can lead to vitamin deficiencies, which those under high levels of stress can ill afford.

As the following story shows, the stress of caregiving can even be fatal.

Tom had a severely disabling stroke when he was 72 years old. He was paralyzed on his right side, wheelchair bound, and he couldn't speak. He also had chronic pain in his legs that was not helped by medication. He often cried out in pain and needed a great deal of comforting.

His wife, Doris, was 65 and worked at a job she had held for the past fifteen years. After Tom came home from the hospital, she tried to continue working. They not only needed the money for Tom's increased medical expenses, Doris enjoyed work immensely. She found a sense of accomplishment that she had not experienced as a homemaker raising children. Even though Tom went to a day care center 5 days a week, Doris found she now really had two jobs. She had to get up very early to bathe and dress Tom and worked hard again at night to prepare his meals, toilet him frequently, and get him to bed.

Within a year, Doris found it becoming increasingly difficult to hold down her two jobs. She was exhausted and no longer able to concentrate on her work. Doris had a history of high blood pressure, which ran in her family. Until now, medication had kept it under control, but it was no longer helping. She was worried. Her doctor told her she needed to relax, but that was impossible. She decided to retire from her job, to stay home and care for Tom.

After her retirement, Doris became more and more depressed. She had never liked staying at home. She loved Tom but she would have preferred to be out of the house instead of caring for the sick old man he'd become. His constant pain tore at her, and she could do little to relieve it.

Tom and Doris had three sons, two of them living in the area. They were attentive to their parents, visiting frequently and helping with some of the heavy care, like bathing Tom. But Doris was the one responsible, she was always there.

She felt guilty because of her feelings of wanting to flee. She felt it was wrong to want to run away from her duty, and so she tried to become the perfect wife and caregiver— always there, always attentive, always giving.

Doris worked hard at her caregiving role. Her primary focus became her husband and his needs. She stopped seeing friends and spent most of her time alone. She didn't like her isolation, but felt it was the only way. She worried a lot — about Tom, their limited finances, and her health. Her blood pressure wouldn't come down.

About one year after her retirement, Doris suffered a massive stroke. She was completely paralyzed and semi-comatose for about four months, until she died. For the next two years, first a son, then a live-in homemaker, cared for Tom at home. Then Tom entered a nursing home and died soon after.

Coping with Emotional and Physical Problems

It is easy to say that caregivers should get emotional support, rest, eat properly, and find time to relax or take a vacation. But caregivers are often overwhelmed by the day-to-day demands, and frequently give up their own needs for rest to meet these demands. Some help may be available (this varies with the community), but the caregiver may have to be persistent to find it.

Getting a break from the 24-hour task of caregiving can be very important, whether it is provided by relatives, a paid attendant, or a day care center. Support from a group or counseling can help alleviate the stress of caregiving and reduce the damaging effects on the caregiver's health. Coping with the heavy load of caregiving is hard to bear alone. More and more communities are developing programs that may help. In Chapter 7, these programs are described in greater detail; the Resources section tells how to get started in finding them. With outside help, a caregiver can better cope with her situation.

Many caregivers find, at some point, that they are being pushed beyond their physical and mental limits. Paid home care, adult day care, or a nursing home may be the only alternatives if the caregiver wants to keep her own health. Sometimes it takes an outside perspective to help the caregiver see that this point has been reached. Jill decided to move out of her home and have a paid attendant move in. She did this, however, only after her doctor advised her that her own health would suffer if she didn't come up with a solution for Ben's care other than doing it all herself. Paula hired a paid attendant only after a visiting nurse told her Gene needed more care than Paula was providing, particularly care that involved lifting, which Paula wasn't able to do. The day-to-day round of tasks can absorb so much attention that the caregiver isn't able to see that she has reached her own limits.

Physical and mental problems brought on by caregiving are a warning to the caregiver that she is trying to do too much. They are also, especially in cases like that of Doris, a warning that society is asking too much of caregivers. They are a symptom of society's deserting caregivers, leaving them to struggle alone, with insufficient resources.

The emotional and physical burdens of caregiving are heavy enough by themselves. But many caregivers are shocked to learn how great the financial costs can be. In the next chapter, we turn to another occupational hazard of caregiving: poverty.

3

The Economics of Caregiving:
Why Caregiving Wives End Up in Poverty

"I can't live a normal life anymore. I'm hardly getting by. If I step out of line just one little bit, if I even buy a pair of shoes, I've got to make sure I have that extra. I didn't have to live that way when he was home. But now, the nursing home has to be paid. If this goes on another two years, I'll be broke. I'll be right down to nothing. I never could have made it without this subsidized apartment. It's less than half what we paid before. But I've had to give up my nice home and store my furniture. I mean, not having a home or even my own furniture in my old age!"

—Edith

(. . .who cared for her husband at home
for three years. He has Alzheimer's
and is now in a nursing home.)

Most caregivers are shocked to learn how little financial help is provided by health insurance or Medicare and how much they must pay for themselves. Caring for someone who is chronically ill over a long period can be very expensive.

Adult children and siblings may spend a great deal of money on care. Their spending is voluntary because the law does not take their incomes and assets into account when considering if the person they are caring for can receive public benefits such as Medicaid. The situation of a caregiving wife is quite different. The way the system is set up today, caregiving often means that a wife faces living the rest of her life in poverty, regardless of her former financial status. When a husband becomes disabled, his wife often pays for the rest of her days. Many former care-givers said they were willing to take on the task, but they bitterly resent the poverty that followed.

Many of the women presently caring for disabled husbands have been lifelong homemakers, with no income or pensions in their own names. But even wives who do have income or a pension share much of the fate of non-working wives. A wife who is working when her husband becomes disabled will face enormous pressures to quit work and stay home with him, especially if she doesn't earn a high salary. Doing so will certainly mean that she loses income in the present. It may also mean that she loses pension or Social Security income in the future. Regardless of whether or not she is able to hold onto her job, *her* income and assets are counted when her disabled husband applies for Medicaid benefits for his care, which, as we shall see, often becomes necessary.

As an example, consider Sam and Martha, a couple in their mid-60s. Sam's federal civil service pension was $600 per month, Martha's Social Security benefit was $300 per month, and their $50,000 bank certificate of deposit gave them interest income of $500 per month. Because they owned their home (valued at around $100,000), their total income of $1,400 per month was minimally adequate. When Sam had a stroke that left him unable to walk or speak, Martha began to care for him at home. She quickly learned that neither Medicare nor their supplemental health insurance policy were much help once Sam came home from the hospital. She was able to get Medicare to pay for a home health agency to send someone to provide periodic physical therapy and to give Sam injections, but only for a short time.

No other home care was covered by Medicare or their supplemental health insurance policy. This is a common problem because both Medicare and most insurance policies make a distinction between what they call "acute" and "custodial" care. Only acute care is covered, and by this they mean medical care to cure or improve the status of a patient during an acute illness. The long period of care after a stroke patient has been "stabilized" is considered custodial.

Martha could not even afford to hire someone to come in and watch Sam while she shopped, kept medical appoint-ments, or went to her granddaughter's first birthday party. She cared for Sam alone, 24 hours a day, until she had a mild heart attack a year later. Her physician said she should take it as a warning, and that it was time for Sam to go into a nursing home.

But there wasn't enough money. While Sam and Martha could get by on $1,400 a month when Sam was at home, they couldn't affort the cost of the nursing home, which was $2,000 per month. Neither Medicare nor Sam's supplemental insurance policy covered any of it, either. Again, this was because both Medicare and the insurance company defined Sam's care in the nursing home as custodial rather than acute. Martha was especially shocked that her health insurance policy didn't cover the nursing home, since she had bought it because she thought it did. She later learned that most insurance policies do not cover nursing home care, though more of them are becoming available.

Martha looked into Medicaid. Medicaid does pay for nursing home care, but only for the very poor. She was appalled to learn that for Sam to qualify for Medicaid, they could have no more than $2,500 in savings (the amount varies from state to state). That meant she would have to spend their savings of $50,000 before he would become eligible. Once that money was gone, they would no longer have the interest income ($500 per month) to live on.

Their total monthly income would then be $900 (Sam's pension plus Martha's Social Security), of which Martha would be allowed to keep about $500 for herself. (In other states, Medicaid would expect her to pay as much as $600 per month out of that on Sam's care, leaving her only $300 to live on herself.) Medicaid would then pay for the remainder of the cost of Sam's nursing home care.

Medicaid is designed as a welfare program; people are allowed to receive benefits only if they are very poor. For Sam to qualify for Medicaid coverage for his nursing home care, Martha's and Sam's income would have to be reduced to below the level of SSI (the federally-funded income support program for people over 65 who have very low or no incomes and very little savings).

Martha also looked into Medicaid payments for home care for Sam. She hoped that Medicaid might pay part of the cost of home care, particularly if it were less expensive than a nursing home and she still provided most of the care. But in her state, Medicaid would pay for care only if Sam went into a nursing home. (In some states Medicaid pays for limited home care, but rarely when there is a full-time caregiver in the home.)

Martha could see a bleak future for herself after Sam's death. Since their savings would have been spent, she would no longer have $500 in interest income each month. And she would no longer receive his $600 civil service pension. (Like so many couples, they had chosen not to have Sam's pension pay a survivor's benefit because that would have meant lower monthly income while he was alive.) Though Medicaid did not require Martha to sell her house as long as she lived in it (either while Sam was in the nursing home or after his death), Martha knew she couldn't pay taxes and insurance on the home with her small Social Security income. But if she sold the house and rented an apartment for herself, Sam would not be eligible for Medicaid until all proceeds from the sale of the house had been spent. While caring for Sam at home might cost Martha her life, putting him in a nursing home meant that the rest of her life would be spent in poverty.

In an attempt to shelter savings, property, or other liquid assets from the Medicaid "spend down" requirement, some people transfer them to other relatives, such as adult children. While this sometimes works, it is risky. Medicaid is considered to be a welfare program, and hiding ownership of assets is illegal; people who are caught can be prosecuted.

In a number of states, a transfer of assets must be completed two years before the person applies for Medicaid. In addition, the caregiver must have a high degree of trust in the person she transfers the assets to, because there is no legal way to make sure that person will later give them back. A written contract saying the adult child would do so is illegal.

In theory, a caregiver could put savings or other liquid assets in an adult child's name more than two years before her husband needed nursing home care. (Then she would not have to "spend them down" for him to receive Medicaid benefits.) After his death, the adult child could return the assets to her.

An attorney should be consulted about such a transfer because sheltering assets in this way carries such heavy risk.

Although it broke her heart, Martha asked an attorney about a divorce. She had learned that this is a way that many caregivers are able to avoid future poverty. Since they lived in a community property state, she could keep half of their community property. But the attorney explained that in Martha's case, this would not really be helpful. Although she could keep one-half of their $50,000 in savings, she would have to give up one-half the value of their $100,000 house. Sam would have $25,000 (half of their savings) and be entitled to $50,000 (half the cash value of the house). All Sam's money (except for $1,700) would have to be spent on nursing home care before he would become eligible for Medicaid.

Because Martha was relatively sophisticated in legal matters, she sought out an attorney with experience in Medicaid eligibility. She found that a new state law allowed her and Sam to execute a "separation of assets" agreement, which would make her half of their community property her own separate property. This is not the same as a marital separation and carries no implication of martial breakdown, which was important to Sam and Martha. Fortunately, Sam's mind was clear enough for him to understand and sign the agreement.

Even with the separation of assets agreement (which is not yet available in most states), Martha's economic future would still not be easy. Her monthly income after Sam's death would be $550 ($300 from Social Security plus $250 interest from her share of their savings).

Unlike a divorce, the agreement allowed Martha to keep her house. As long as she lived in it, Medicaid would not count it as an asset while Sam was in a nursing home. After his death, she could sell it, buy a less expensive home, and use the difference as income. (If she did this while Sam was still alive, however, in most states the money would have to be spent for Sam's care before Medicaid would begin to pay.)

Caregiving wives face tragic and unjust choices. In the following two sections, we will first outline the current ways caregivers may find help in paying for a disabled relative's long-term care. Second, we will describe techniques for protecting the caregiving wife's income. But these are only Band-Aids. The economic problems caregivers face cannot be solved under the present system. What is necessary is coverage of long-term care under either Medicaid or Medicare without the caregiving wife having to reach the poverty level herself.

Paying for Care

Aside from Medicaid, with its requirement of impoverishment, neither the public nor the private sector offers much protection from the expenses of chronic, disabling illness. Some limited financial help may come from Medicare, private health insurance, supplemental coverage to Medicare, disability insurance, supplemental medical coverage, the Veterans Administration, or tax breaks. A few special programs also help a small number of caregivers with their expenses.

Medicare

Medicare is designed to help pay the medical bills of people 65 and over and of those under 65 who have been disabled for two years or more. It is not based on need, and it is currently financed by payroll taxes, general revenues, and premiums paid by participants. In addition, participants pay a share of cost through deductibles and co-payments. Medicare's share of the health costs of the elderly has been declining since its inception two decades ago; it now covers less than one-half of the total health care costs of people over 65.

The major problem affecting caregivers is that Medicare excludes what it defines as "custodial care." Although a substantial majority of Americans believe that Medicare pays for nursing home care, the fact is that it only pays around 2 percent of the nation's nursing home costs. Medicare pays for *skilled* nursing care, but most nursing home care is not skilled and therefore ineligible for Medicare payments. Moreover, even for skilled nursing care in a nursing home, Medicare pays for a maximum of 100 days, with the patient paying a substantial part of the cost for 80 of those days.

To qualify for home health care in the Medicare program, a patient must meet three tests: he or she must (1) be "home-bound," (2) need "intermittent" nursing care, and (3) need "skilled" nursing care, not merely custodial or homemaking care. Increasingly, homebound is being interpreted as "bedbound," so that those patients who achieve any mobility within or outside the home are disqualified for Medicare payment. Patients have failed the "intermittent" test when the physician has ordered home nursing services three or five days per week and have been denied under the "skilled" test when Medicare authorities have determined that the care could be performed by untrained relatives or friends.

Even patients who qualify for Medicare coverage of home care find there is a diabolical "catch-22." They can become disqualified for Medicare coverage if they supplement it with additional home care paid by other funds, such as Medicaid, private insurance, or even private savings. The reasoning is that the additional services prove the need is more than intermittent, and therefore not covered by Medicare in the first place.

Recent congressional concern over "catastrophic" health costs under Medicare may promise some relief. Pending bills do not propose Medicare coverage of custodial long-term care. But they do contain provisions to loosen current restrictions on home health coverage, provide some respite care coverage, and protect some of a couple's life savings and monthly income from the Medicaid spend-down.

Medicaid

Medicaid is a welfare program. In contrast to Medicare, it will cover long-term custodial expenses for a person who is 65, blind, or disabled, but only if that person has assets of less than $1,700 - $3,400 (depending on the state and whether the person is married or not) and only if the monthly income after medical costs is no higher than the level of the state's SSI benefits (generally well below poverty level).

The home where the disabled person lives is not counted in computing the assets. The spouse may continue to live in the home after the disabled person has entered a nursing home without it counting as part of the assets for Medicaid purposes; however, Medicaid establishes a lien against the home after the death of the couple.

Medicaid has a strong bias toward nursing home care, rather than care at home or at day health care centers. In about twenty states, Medicaid will pay only for nursing home care for people it classes as "medically needy," people who have an income higher than the poverty level but whose medical bills leave them below the poverty level. In other states, a person who meets the income requirements may qualify for Medicaid coverage for services such as the restricted home health care benefits noted earlier and adult day care.

Medicaid pays almost 50 percent of the nation's nursing home bills, and nearly 70 percent of people in nursing homes receive Medicaid. In most states Medicaid pays nursing homes considerably less than the rates charged private paying patients. Naturally, this creates a preference for private paying patients, which, in turn, explains the rampant discrimination against Medicaid patients in admissions, services, transfers, and discharges.

As previously described, in order to receive help from Medicaid for either care at home or in a nursing home, a couple has to have spent all their savings down to the small amount Medicaid allows them to keep. If a wife has been paying for her husband's nursing home care before he becomes eligible for Medicaid, she may find that the nursing home he is in will not keep him once Medicaid is paying the bill, but may "dump" him (illegally) in a less desirable facility.

After he dies, the caregiver faces poverty for the rest of her life. Although Medicaid is the only program that will pay a substantial portion of the cost of a nursing home, its requirement of impoverishment makes it a less than ideal solution for most caregivers.

Private Health Insurance

In the U.S. nearly all private health insurance is group insurance tied to employment. A person with a disabling disease may not be covered. A man who becomes progressively disabled by Alzheimer's or Parkinson's, or suddenly disabled by a stroke, may lose his job. Losing the job means eventually losing group health coverage. A new federal law allows people to remain in the group policy for 18 months after they lose a job, but the cost to the individual is high (between $1,000 and $2,000 per year in many cases). Once someone with a chronic illness has lost group health coverage, there is little chance of obtaining individual coverage, although a handful of states require carriers to provide expensive, no-frills policies.

Some organizations offer association group health coverage to their members. An otherwise uninsurable person might qualify for "excess major medical coverage," a type of policy that usually carries a $25,000 or $50,000 deductible. Although this is an enormous sum, it does put an upper limit on hospital expenses. It can mean that the dimensions of a possible medical catastrophe are at least known, and it may be possible to set aside the amount of the deductible in savings. Such a policy can offer security against loss of the home, or other nightmare scenarios a caregiver may contemplate.

Most insurance policies have "exclusions." Therefore, even if the ill person qualifies for new insurance, the policy will almost surely not cover any costs arising from the illness. Because people with one health problem are likely to develop another, it is still worthwhile to buy an otherwise sound policy even with exclusions for pre-existing conditions. Shopping around is important; some policies limit the exclusion to one or two years, although this may be buried in the fine print.

Finally, a "hospital indemnity" policy in the name of the incapacitated person should be considered if no other insurance is available. These policies pay, typically, $50 to $100 per day toward hospital costs. They are not recommended for anyone eligible for better coverage, but a caregiver can purchase several in her husband's name and know she will have $400 to $500 per day if he is hospitalized. One caution: many banks, department stores, and credit companies offer indemnity policies at very low rates. A close reading often reveals that these policies are limited to hospitalization for accidents only, or for some specific disease, such as cancer.

If the relative is eligible for insurance, the caregiver must make sophisticated judgments in a very technical field. Generally, health maintenance organizations (HMOs) provide the broadest range of services at by far the lowest rate. They are not available in many parts of the country, however, and some are available only through employment. Blue Cross/Blue Shield coverage is widely available, but not everyone qualifies. Although most commercial carriers offer excellent group coverage, it is seldom available to individuals. When it is, individual coverage is expensive and covers less than group coverage.

Even the best insurance coverage will not cover many services a disabled person needs. Like Medicare, private health insurance ordinarily covers only acute medical care. Extended home care coverage is rare; when offered, it is strictly for skilled procedures. Health insurance will not pay for adult day care, for respite care, or for help with chores. The grinding routine—

where the caregiver changes the bedding three times a day and damages her own health lifting, dressing, and bathing her relative — is all beyond the scope of health insurance coverage. These policies rarely cover nursing home care. Insurance to cover long-term care is still in its earliest experimental stages, and not available in all areas.

Caregivers walk a fine line. Some, in panic, err on the side of too much coverage, buying single disease and accidental dismemberment policies with small chance of ever getting benefits from them. Others "go bare" for lack of information on how to patch together coverage that would at least stave off disaster. A caregiver's own insurance coverage is as important as the ill person's, since the strain she is under may make her more prone to illness. She must make sophisticated decisions in the minefield of health coverage. And because long-term care is so rarely covered, she often finds that health insurance, even if she can buy it, will not protect her from spending herself into poverty.

Supplemental Coverage to Medicare

Once a person qualifies for Medicare, either because of passing age 65 or due to long-term disability, the problem of health insurance is less serious. Although Medicare pays less than half the medical costs of people it covers (due to premiums, deductibles, and co-payments), it is a welcome haven when compared to no coverage at all.

The health insurance industry has responded to the opportunities presented by the "gaps" in Medicare coverage. Medicare supplement, or "medi-gap," policies abound, including offerings from Blue Cross, Blue Shield, HMOs, and commercial carriers. They are generally available without a medical examination and have limited exclusions for pre-existing conditions.

In general, these policies share the same problems of other health insurance policies. They, too, will not cover custodial care, whether in a home or nursing home.

Some policies promise nursing home coverage, but in all but a few, this promise is an illusion. In obscure language, the policy usually states it will pay for only the nursing home care that Medicare covers. The catch is that almost *no* nursing home care qualifies for payment under Medicare. Medicare pays only for "skilled nursing care" and it only covers (in part) the first 100 days. The average length of a Medicare-covered stay is two weeks; very few conditions require more than 100 days of skilled nursing home care. Therefore, in most cases the promise of nursing home care coverage in a supplemental policy is misleading.

Nursing home or long-term care insurance is now becoming widely available in most of the United States. These insurance policies offer a wide range of coverages, but the restrictions and limitations in the fine print tend to reduce their real value. Unfortunately, at the present time consumers in most states have little protection against substandard policies and misrepresentation in marketing.

Disability Insurance

Disability insurance may provide income that can help pay for care. Some employers provide disability insurance, through either state plans or private carriers. Generally, though, people over 65 cannot be covered, even if they are employed. Of course, after the disability occurs it is too late to purchase insurance for it.

Anytime there is disability insurance, the caregiver should follow through on all claims. State disability plans are short-term; private carrier plans vary in duration. No plan pays benefits after the death of the disabled person.

Veterans Benefits

If the parent or husband being cared for was in the military, the Veterans Administration may offer some services. The VA has a network of hospitals, nursing homes, and clinics across the country. Special programs are available to certain categories of veterans, such as former prisoners of war, those with service-connected disabilities and those who were exposed to atomic radiation. The VA provides some respite care, adult day care and home health care. Not all programs are available in all locations. Veterans who are not retired from military careers generally must meet income requirements, and those whose disability is not connected with military service may not be eligible.

Tax Breaks

Although the present tax system provides very little help to caregivers, every caregiver should take advantage of the help that is provided. A caregiver who is also employed outside the home is eligible for a federal income tax credit to partly offset the costs of paid substitute care for a disabled adult as well as for a child. If a husband is in a nursing home, his care is deductible as a medical expense on federal income taxes. State income tax systems may allow similar credits, deductions, and exemptions.

Other Programs

Some communities offer services to caregivers, such as respite care or paid attendants, free or on a sliding fee scale. These services may be sponsored by nonprofit groups, local government agencies, or churches. They are far from widely available.

The federal government, under Title XX of the Social Security Act, provides some help with personal care and household tasks to ill or disabled people with very low monthly incomes who might otherwise have to live in a nursing home. These services are available only if monthly income is no more than the level of Supplemental Security Income (SSI) benefits or if large medical bills reduce the income to that level. In some states, a person with a caregiver in the home is not eligible.

Planning for the Caregiver's Future

Even with good health plan coverage, the caregiver cannot rely on either public or private health carriers for the expenses she faces. Worse yet, her future income may be reduced to the poverty level. Though it is not possible under the present system to make sure she is not forced to become poor, there are ways that a caregiver may be able to protect her future income. Possible sources of income a caregiver can take into account in her planning include pensions, Social Security, IRAs, insurance, savings, reverse mortgages, and welfare.

Pensions

Many a widow learns only at her husband's funeral that the pension they have been living on was buried with him. Pension plans are not required to keep paying benefits to a spouse after the pensioner dies. Generally, a retiring employee is offered a choice between receiving benefits during his or her lifetime or receiving a lower monthly amount plus a monthly "survivor's benefit" for the spouse after the retiree dies.

In the past, a husband could choose the option of receiving higher benefits during his lifetime without even telling his wife. A new federal law now requires a spouse to give written consent before her survivor's benefit is signed away.

Rules for pension plans vary. If a husband becomes disabled before retirement, there's a good chance that he will forfeit his pension. If a man becomes disabled and dies before retirement age, his widow may still be able to collect pension benefits, but generally not until the date her husband would have reached retirement age, and only if he worked at the pension-covered job for more than ten years.

A caregiver must be very practical about her own future. If her husband's pension is already "vested" at the time he becomes disabled, but the choice about type of benefit has not been made, the couple should choose to receive a survivor's benefit, even though it means a lower monthly pension during the husband's lifetime. When the couple has already selected to forgo the survivor's benefit, there is probably little that can be done; almost no pension plan will permit a change of heart. It is worth checking, of course. If the caregiver discovers that she will not receive a survivor's benefit, she should seriously consider maintaining any life insurance her husband has, even if it is expensive.

Social Security

If a couple is already receiving Social Security retirement benefits when the husband becomes disabled, there will be no change in the amount they receive. However, Social Security is not just a retirement program, it also protects against the loss of income because of disability. An employee covered by Social Security who becomes disabled before age 62 may be eligible for disability benefits. The wife of a disabled recipient can also receive spouse benefits when she is age 62 (or younger, if she is caring for his dependent children).

If she waits until age 65 to collect benefits, she will get full retirement benefits. At age 65, a dependent spouse receives benefits equal to half of her husband's benefit; the amount doubles after his death. But if she begins collecting benefits earlier (as early as age 62 as a spouse or age 60 as a widow), the checks will be permanently reduced to take into account the longer period of time she will collect.

Social Security doesn't have the same traps as pensions; there's no way to forfeit a survivor's benefit, for example. However, regulations are complex and changing. For example, under the Reagan administration, many claims for disability have been denied. Any time this happens, it is worth pursuing the Social Security appeals procedure. A large proportion of initial decisions denying disability benefits are overturned at the hearing level (one step beyond the "review" level). It is very important at the outset to engage an attorney who has experience in Social Security disability appeals.

Legal help is sometimes available at low or no cost (see page 88 for advice on how to locate legal help). Private attorneys may also be willing to take on Social Security claims appeals on a *contingency* basis. This means the caregiver pays no legal fees until she wins the case, at which time the government will pay a portion of her award to her attorney.

IRAs

Many caregivers are unaware that their husband's Individual Retirement Account (IRA) can be tapped before he is 59 1/2, without penalty, if he becomes disabled. By spending this money, the caregiver will reduce her future income. On the other hand, if the couple tries to become eligible for Medicaid to pay for nursing home care, Medicaid will require that all the funds in the IRA be included in the assets that must be spend down before Medicaid will begin to pay for the care.

Life Insurance

An insurance policy on her husband's life will guarantee some future income for a caregiving wife after the death of her disabled husband. It will be difficult to obtain life insurance coverage after the onset of his disability, but it still may be possible to obtain group life insurance from club memberships or even department store charge accounts. The cash value of a "whole life" insurance policy counts as an asset as far as Medicaid benefits are concerned, and must be "spent down" before the disabled husband qualifies. Term life insurance, which does not build up a cash value, but only pays when the insured person dies, does not count as an asset. However, a caregiver might find it difficult (or impossible) to keep up payments on a term insurance policy on the income she is allowed to keep under Medicaid. If Medicaid funding for nursing home care is sought, neither form of insurance is likely to survive as an asset.

Savings

Savings, as we have seen in the example of Sam and Martha, can be rapidly depleted by caregiving. In some states, half the couple's savings may be reserved for the caregiving wife's use through a "separation of assets."

Reverse Mortgages

A "reverse mortgage" allows a couple who own a home to receive monthly income from a bank while they are still living in the home. The bank gradually acquires a lien against the home. A couple desperately trying to stay afloat may be tempted to tap this resource.

But, again, this means cannibalizing the future income of the caregiver to meet the present needs of the disabled husband. Most reverse mortgage contracts entitle the bank to foreclose on the home, usually after ten years.

Another consideration: since a home is the only large asset not taken into account if the caregiver must ever apply for Medicaid or other welfare benefits, converting it to cash while her husband is alive can only make her even poorer later on. If the home is not tapped for income, she will at least have it to live in if the time for welfare comes, preserving some part of her former lifestyle.

Welfare

It is poor public policy indeed that permits—or worse, requires—the permanent impoverishment of the spouse of a severely disabled person. Nonetheless, many caregivers will learn that the nation's welfare programs are their last resort.

Supplemental Security Income (SSI) pays a small monthly income to the needy disabled, the aged (over 65), and those who are blind. For a caregiver or widow to qualify, her income and assets must be very low. Aid to Families with Dependent Children (AFDC) is a similar program, for poor families with a child under age 18. If a person fits neither of these categories, only general assistance may be available; this program may pay as little as $100 per month.

A caregiver who is under 60, not blind or severely disabled, with no children in her home, can find herself in the most vulnerable situation our society affords. And she is in this position only because she has suffered the catastrophe of her husband's illness.

A caregiver may have to steel herself to make some hard decisions. Against her natural inclination, she must make her future life as high a priority as the present crisis. And even if she has the time, energy, and resources to analyze and maximize every possible source of future income, she still may not be able to prevent a deeply impoverished old age.

But it does not have to be this way. In Chapters 8 and 9, we propose changes in public policy that would mean caregiving wives would not face their enormous tasks alone with the risk of poverty on top of it all. Society needs to be in partnership with caregivers. Caregivers need to be able to live out their lives in dignity, with adequate income. And protecting caregivers' assets now may actually save taxpayers money later—in the years of welfare benefits that will not have to be paid.

4

When the Law Becomes Part of the Picture: Managing the Affairs of Others

At age 82, Susan slipped on her front steps and broke her hip. After three weeks in the hospital, her doctor told her she was ready to leave, but not well enough to live alone in her own home. Susan was discharged to the home of her younger sister, Mary. At first, it was a temporary arrangement, but both women gradually realized that Susan would never be able to go back to living on her own. Susan had two grown sons. As in many families, however, the sons did not take much direct responsibility for Susan's care. Susan ended up living with Mary indefinitely.

One of the many new problems Mary and Susan had to face was the question of how to handle Susan's finances. Susan couldn't leave the house to go to the bank or to sign for certified mail at the post office. But she wanted to keep managing her own affairs and was mentally able to do so. She only needed a pair of legs, and Mary was ready and willing to provide them. So Susan wrote a letter on her personal stationery authorizing Mary to sign on her behalf.

The letter worked at the post office. But when Mary took it to Susan's bank and to her savings and loan, they refused to honor it. Mary and Susan suddenly found themselves in a thicket of legal questions:

Should Susan add Mary's name to all her accounts?

Should Susan execute a power of attorney?

Should they set up a trust, conservatorship, or guardianship?

Caregivers often face new and unfamiliar problems with the law. People who become physically or mentally disabled will require some assistance with their financial affairs. The law provides an array of devices for managing another person's affairs.

A spouse may manage to make both financial and health decisions for a disabled person without resorting to any of these devices. A relative like Mary, however, will need some device that will allow her to act for Susan in her financial affairs. A spouse or other relative may need to be given authority to make health care decisions. A caregiver who isn't related—a friend or "significant other"—absolutely needs a legal device for both health and financial decisions.

These legal devices have a broad range of cost, effectiveness, and inconvenience. When the only problem is physical, as in the example of Mary and Susan, a caregiver may want to select the device she can set up most quickly and easily. If mental competency should ever become an issue, though, the question of which device to use can be crucial. It's not always easy to decide which device to use, and not all devices are available in every state. All of them require some degree of advance planning. It may be very helpful to consult with an attorney.

Co-Signing Accounts

At first, Mary thought the easiest way to proceed would be having her name added as "co-signer" to Susan's checking and savings accounts. She assumed (as most people would) that the accounts would still be Susan's. But legally, something quite different takes place. Mary would become either a *joint tenant* or a *tenant in common* with Susan on the accounts, and the bank might not even tell her which she became.

As a joint tenant, she could, if she wanted to, spend all the money in the accounts for her own use, and Susan would have to sue Mary to get it back. If Susan were to die, all the money in the accounts would become Mary's, even though Susan's will directed part of it to someone else. Tax authorities might at some point decide that Susan had given Mary a taxable gift. Worst of all, Mary's creditors could attach the account.

Mary was debt-free and had no intention of spending Susan's money on herself. But if she were someday found liable in an unforeseen accident, what had formerly been Susan's assets could be taken to pay damages. In other words, if Mary became a joint tenant as a co-signer of Susan's accounts, she would acquire legal right to them, and so would her creditors.

Sometimes joint tenancy is preferred so that the caregiver can avoid probate, a complicated and expensive legal proceeding, after the disabled person's death.

The other way to assume co-ownership of a bank account is called "tenancy in common." A tenant in common owns a specified share of the account. Mary and Susan could arrange for Mary to own 5 percent of the tenancy in common and Susan, 95 percent. Then Mary's creditors could reach no more than her 5 percent and Susan's will would determine what would happen to her 95 percent after she died.

Tenancy in common serves its purpose in that Mary's signature would still be valid for withdrawing amounts larger than 5 percent of the account.

Either joint tenancy or tenancy in common can be an appropriate device; it all depends on the situation. Either one should be used only with competent legal advice and only if the caregiver understands all the legal implications.

Power of Attorney

Mary and Susan decided to avoid the pitfalls of co-owner-ships. Instead, they chose a *power of attorney*. Mary bought a standard power of attorney form at a stationery store, Susan signed it, and they had it notarized. The power of attorney allowed Mary to sign checks, contracts, and other legal documents for Susan.

Susan still owned all her assets; Mary suffered no tax consequences. Susan's will determined who would inherit her accounts, and Mary's creditors could not attach Susan's accounts.

However, Susan's bank and her savings and loan refused to honor the document Mary bought at the stationery store. Each wanted them to sign several different forms, which all had to be notarized. Arranging power of attorney was a hassle, but eventually it was accomplished. And, for a time, the power of attorney seemed the perfect tool for Mary and Susan's purposes.

Soon, however, Mary discovered that new legal pitfalls arise when the person being cared for becomes mentally incompetent. These are common traps for caregivers and they are almost certain consequences of chronic diseases that involve loss of mental faculties. Caregivers (and even more often, the people they care for) don't like to face what happens when mental abilities start to go. But, as Mary learned, failure to plan for mental incompetency can cause major problems.

All states allow power of attorney, and anyone can hold this power; it is not necessary to be related to the person granting the power. It is only necessary that the person signing the power of attorney be mentally competent. A married caregiver might need to get power of attorney from her husband if the couple holds assets separately or if any of their community property is held in his name alone. Since arranging for power of attorney is more trouble than it is for co-signing on bank accounts, a caregiver may not want to resort to it if co-signing can meet her needs and those of the person she cares for.

Incompetency and Durable Power of Attorney

Susan began to have periods when her thinking and memory were cloudy. Her doctor was unable to determine the cause. Gradually, she became less and less able to take care of her finances.

When a person becomes mentally incompetent, an ordinary power of attorney is no longer legally valid. But Mary didn't know this. She knew that Susan was not going to be able to move back to her own house, so Mary put it up for sale. It was sold, and Mary recorded the deed and the power of attorney. Then Susan's sons challenged the sale, saying that Mary didn't have the power to act because Susan had become incompetent. Mary was soon involved in litigation with the disappointed buyers and her nephews.

Incompetency is a gray area of the law. There is no legal litmus test that clearly defines it. Consequently, it is hard to be sure whether a power of attorney is valid or not. Every state now provides a *durable* power of attorney, which continues after the person becomes incompetent. The durable power of attorney is an excellent option for any aging person, whether or not he or she has been diagnosed with a disease that can include loss of mental abilities. Should competency become a factor in the future, the person will have designated someone who will be able to handle his or her financial affairs.

Durable powers of attorney are useful in many situations, in addition to that of siblings like Susan and Mary. They would probably be the device of choice for a wife or daughter of a person who became mentally incompetent. For example, a wife could not sell property that was in the couple's names, or in her husband's name, if the husband became mentally incompetent to sign. She would need a durable power of attorney or one of the more cumbersome devices described later in this chapter.

A variation is the *"springing" durable power of attorney*, which only becomes effective *after* the person becomes incompetent. Springing durable powers of attorney are now available in the majority of states. The caregiver can't decide on her own to use the "springing" power; a legal or medical determination must be made first (who makes it varies by state). This gives the person turning over control of his or her affairs more power than with a durable power of attorney, where there is no automatic court supervision and therefore a risk of abuse.

While it takes some foresight and sophistication about the law to have one of these documents signed in time, it can save a lot of problems later on. The document must be signed while the person is legally competent.

Another useful legal tool is the *durable power of attorney for health care*, which allows the designated person to make decisions about the other person's health if that person were unable to make them. It is available in all fifty states and the District of Columbia. Without it, what can happen varies from state to state. A minority of states have laws designating the closest kin to make such decisions for a person who can't make them. For Susan, that would be her sons, and not Mary. Other states have no law. Doctors might informally consult Mary regarding Susan's care, but she couldn't count on it.

As with other powers of attorney, a durable power of attorney for health care must be signed while the patient is mentally competent. A durable power of attorney for health care is frequently necessary, and usually a good idea, even if the caregiver is the closest relative of the person being cared for. If the caregiver is a more distant relative, a friend, or a lesbian partner, it is a necessity.

Susan continued living with Mary, but she became less and less able to manage her finances. She also required much more care, and Mary hired a home health aide to help her. To help pay for the home health aide, Mary decided to move Susan's savings from a 5 percent passbook account into a 10 percent money market account. While Susan was still legally competent she had refused to do this, because she was a cautious saver. Unfortunately, even the durable power of attorney did not allow Mary to act outside of Susan's known wishes (while she was still competent). Mary would be acting improperly and Susan's sons could object if they found out.

Living Trusts

There is another device that gives a caregiver like Mary management powers over Susan's finances—more than just the authority to carry out Susan's express wishes, as with a durable power of attorney. It is called a *revocable inter-vivos (living) trust.* It may also be used, when a person anticipates incompetency, to avoid conservatorship (see below), although a durable power of attorney can also serve this purpose.

Susan could have put her house and checking and savings accounts into a living trust. Even more than a durable power of attorney, a living trust requires planning and legal sophistication, and involves legal fees, careful bookkeeping, termination formalities and fees, and, in some states, an accounting after the person dies. It, too, must be set up while the person is still mentally competent.

Co-ownerships, powers of attorney, and living trusts require foresight, and a caregiver should consult an attorney to determine which is best.

Conservatorship

Sometimes, when a person suddenly becomes disabled and legally incompetent (as with a stroke or in an accident, for example) the caregiver may not have the opportunity to exercise the options given above. A caregiver facing a relative's gradual mental deterioration may not recognize the legal implication. An older person experiencing a gradually worsening disability may not want to face what is happening, and so may refuse to sign the legal document during the time he or she is still competent.

Once the person is legally incompetent, the caregiver faced with managing the person's financial affairs must turn to the most cumbersome legal alternative: the *conservatorship* or *guardianship*. The terms are somewhat used interchangeably and definitions vary by state. Here, we will use the more modern term, conservatorship.

In general, a conservatorship gives someone else (a "conservator") very broad powers: the power to manage financial affairs and make financial decisions for a person who is mentally unable to do so, and also control over personal decisions, such as whether to enter a nursing home or consent to medical treatment. Impaired people don't necessarily need to surrender control over both of these areas. Sometimes an impaired person may have someone else appointed to handle financial transactions, but may still be able to make medical decisions, such as whether to have surgery.

A caregiver may feel her relative needs to be moved to the caregiver's home or to a nursing home, and the relative may refuse. For example, a parent who lives alone may contract Alzheimer's disease. Eventually, the parent's behavior may become dangerous (leaving the stove on, for example), but the parent may refuse to recognize it. In this case, a conservatorship of the person is the only legal device that will give the caregiver power to move a parent when he or she is unwilling.

Conservatorship may also be required by a hospital when relatives disagree about health care decisions for a person who can't make them. Many conservatorships are initiated because of a title company's insistence.

Because taxes and upkeep on Susan's house were expensive, and because her bank accounts were being drained to pay for her home care, Mary and her nephews (Susan's sons) finally agreed that Susan's house would be sold. By now, Susan was no longer legally competent to sign the papers authorizing the sale. The title company insisted that Mary must be appointed conservator of Susan's assets, in order to convey a clear title.

The procedure might involve an investigator coming to Mary's home to talk to Susan and look at her situation; then Mary would probably have a court hearing before a judge. Judges also occasionally come to hospitals to make determinations for conservatorships.

Conservatorship is a legal device that entails a massive loss of civil rights for the impaired person. There is also considerable loss of dignity in being judged incompetent by a court. The process is costly and can take several months (although temporary orders can be issued quickly). From the viewpoint of a person who may become unable to manage his or her own affairs, it is far better to choose a less restrictive device early in the course of a disease, when the decision is still under his or her control.

Sometimes the impaired person does not agree that he or she needs a conservator, or disagrees with the choice of the person seeking to be appointed. The impaired person could hire a lawyer or might have one appointed by the court. The proposed conservator is also entitled to have a lawyer. The process can be very unpleasant and messy, both for the caregiver and her disabled relative. Occasionally, relatives try to be appointed conservator in order to get the impaired person's money.

A caregiver who loses a contested conservatorship will probably have to cope with the other person who has been named conservator, if the court has appointed one. If the court has ruled that her relative is mentally competent, she can try for one of the less restrictive devices described earlier (though a relative who has just been through the process of fighting conservatorship may not be in a mood to sign anything).

For Mary and Susan, the conservatorship placed Susan's financial decision in Mary's hands. Mary had to make periodic reports to the court, and she was under the direct supervision of a court-appointed social worker.

Not all states have close supervision of conservators by social workers, but all states require some reporting of financial transactions. This is a commendable attempt to restrain any threats to the civil liberties of the disabled person. But compared to the less restrictive devices described earlier, there are real disadvantages to the caregiver. In addition to her other burdens, she has the added expense, hassle, and loss of privacy when a court investigator comes to check on the relative's situation.

Conservatorships and guardianships are valuable and necessary tools. However, they should be used only as a last resort. Co-ownership, power of attorney, and living trust are all less drastic and less cumbersome. Too often, caregivers are pressured by family and friends to opt for conservatorship prematurely, when planning and foresight would allow the use of a more appropriate legal device.

Getting Legal Advice

It is never too early for a caregiver and her disabled relative to seek legal advice. Advance planning can save money and time and can help the caregiver avoid hassles and heartbreaking conflicts with family members.

Finding a good attorney may not be easy, however. The most traditional methods are to ask friends or call the local bar association referral service; neither guarantees quality work or reasonable cost. Calling a woman's bar association may be no better. One source of legal help for people over 60 is the local Senior Services office. The State Department of Aging can provide a referral to this office (see "Resources" for how to locate the state office on aging). A referral to a private attorney of the Senior Legal Services office of trusts might be useful.

The Senior Legal Service office also provides free legal help to people over 60. Local legal aid societies may provide free help to people of any age. However, these offices generally provide only emergency level help to people of low income. Advice on estate planning, trusts, most wills, powers of attorney, and property transfers won't be available free. If private legal help is too expensive, do-it-yourself law books can be helpful. Nolo Press has a list of good how-to books available by writing 950 Parker St., Berkeley, CA 94710.

5

The Anguished Decision:

Opting for the Nursing Home

Helen took care of her husband, Edgar, at home for six years. Edgar's strokes left him in a wheelchair at first, but physical therapy and Helen's patient help got him up and walking. Then, he fell and broke his leg. Recovery was slow. A year later there was another small stroke, and then another.

During Edgar's last year at home, he recognized where he was only intermittently. He was confined to bed and a wheelchair, although he occasionally tried to get up and walk. Helen had to watch him constantly, especially at night, to prevent falling. During that last year, Edgar lost control of his bladder, and then his bowels. The hardest part for Helen was "accepting the fact that he was no longer the person he was. And having to treat him as a child, with his sense of pride and independence." Helen cared for him full-time, with her only help being an aide who came in two afternoons a week. At age 72, she was exhausted and badly needed treatment for her almost constant back pain.

Helen didn't like to even think about the possibility of a nursing home. She felt it would be so unfair to Edgar, that it would be such a sad place for him. But finally, her doctor told her that she was ruining her own health and that she shouldn't put it off any longer. It was time for Edgar to go to a nursing home.

The media myth says that America abandons its elderly to nursing homes. If that myth were true, the population of the nation's nursing homes would be far greater than it is today.

The truth is closer to this: America abandons many of its older women, who are left to care for impaired older relatives entirely on their own. More seriously impaired older people live at home in their communities than live in nursing homes. They are at home because some family member—usually a wife, daughter or daughter-in-law—is giving care.

Many of these women provide care right up until the day their relative dies. But many others reach a time when they have exhausted every alternative, and they have exhausted themselves. Like Helen, they must face a decision that is never easy: the decision to put their relative in a nursing home.

Caregivers who live with their impaired husband or parent usually hold out the longest. Most often, these caregivers are wives, likely to be close in age to their husbands. Although these women are the least able to physically handle the tasks of caregiving, they are often the most emotionally and socially motivated to keep going. Daughters, daughters-in-law and even sisters who share a home with the impaired relative also postpone moving them to a nursing home as long as they can.

Like many women in her situation, Helen didn't make the decision right away. Her son, who lived in another state, was against the idea. "He said I owe it to my husband to keep him here at home. It's anguishing; forty years of marriage and I can't take care of him," she said.

Nursing homes are perceived as dumping grounds; the choice is bound to produce anguish and guilt. It took Helen several months to finally decide. There wasn't any particular "straw that broke the camel's back" for her. She just finally came to agree with her doctor that she was no longer able to go on caring for Edgar.

This is often the way caregivers who live with an impaired relative come to the decision. They will often avoid placement long beyond the time when outsiders would see it as appropriate. With chronic illnesses, conditions change slowly and a caregiver may not perceive the slow decline in her relative or, for that matter, even in herself. She may keep trying to adapt to an increasingly intolerable situation. If the caregiver does realize that her tasks are becoming impossible, she may, nonetheless, attempt to avoid putting her relative in a nursing home because she feels such a strong sense of responsibility.

An outside viewpoint is often crucial, as it was for Helen. Without the opinion of a doctor or other professional, many caregivers would never turn to a nursing home. A relative who is not as involved with day-to-day care may also provide the outside opinion that tips the scales in favor of a nursing home.

When it came to the question of where Edgar could go, Helen was lucky. Her doctor found an excellent facility that could take Edgar. Said Helen, "I now have peace of mind knowing he's where I can see what's happening. It's a good place for him, even though he's not entirely happy. He's in good hands. He sees a nurse every day." Helen was also fortunate that she had the money to pay for Edgar's care.

Like Edgar, many people in nursing homes have been previously cared for at home, often for a long time. Margaret cared for her grandmother, mother, and father— as each, in turn, became disabled—for more than twenty years.

When my youngest child was a year old, my mother was diagnosed as having arteriosclerosis, a disease in which the blood cannot reach the brain because the arteries are clogged. She suffered severe seizures about once a month that left her semi-conscious and nauseous for a week afterward. She referred to these periods as her "blackouts." With each episode, she suffered more brain damage. During these seizures she wet herself and lost control of her bowels. She also bit her tongue if her dentures were not removed. But removing her dentures was difficult because her jaws were clamped shut.

Mother could not be left alone. My father was still employed, so I volunteered to keep her during the day and my father picked her up at night on his way home. This arrangement lasted for five years.

I learned how to anticipate Mother's impending seizures by the change in her mood a few days before. I was ready with diapers and also could sometimes use the ploy of soaking her dentures in a cleaner in order to keep her from biting her tongue. Many times she refused to be "toothless" and I would have to pry her mouth open when it was too late.

Mother required an enormous amount of patience and care, but I never regretted having her. Even though caring for a person whose thinking processes are impaired is extremely trying, I felt she had given me life and now it was my turn to take care of her—besides, I loved her very much.

But it was like having a new baby with the diapering, bed changes, and a special no-sodium, no-fat diet. She also began to preach about her religion for hour upon hour, which became almost unbearable to those around her. She would talk incessantly until one day my husband yelled at her to shut up. She was quiet for a few minutes, then began again. I was so used to it, yet I found it difficult to turn a deaf ear. A more difficult thing for both Mother and me was her problem of impacted bowels. It was a constant battle with enemas and experimental diets. I remember thinking, if I stop and think about all this, I'll go mad myself.

When Margaret's father retired, he cared for his wife for a time. Then,

One night Mother left their home and wandered out on the streets not knowing where she was. The police picked her up and held her in the psychiatric ward of the county hospital. The courts declared her incompetent and sent her to a state hospital for the insane, where conditions were deplorable and dangerous. Even though Mother suffered from a *physical* illness, there was no other facility to administer to her. With the faithful use of her medication and proper diet, she became quite rational and "normal." When her condition improved, I asked for her release to my care.

The incident that led to Margaret's opting for a nursing home was dramatic.

She refused to take her medication, even when I ground it up and hid it in her food. She began having episodes of violence and, during one of these scenes, struck me on the side of the head with a metal statuette. Then she broke the towel rails off the bathroom wall, tore the toilet seat off, and went out the bathroom window. When my teenage son

95

tried to bring her back to the house, she began punching him.

At that moment I realized I no longer had any choice. I called an ambulance and sent her back to the hospital. Taking her medicines by injection, she was soon stabilized. She was then released to a community half-way house, where she began to have falls and eventually was bed-ridden.

Mother remained in a very fine nursing home for four more years. During that time I visited her three times a week to feed her and carefully monitor her care. My oldest son visited her often after school and would lovingly massage her dry skin with lotions he bought for that purpose. We took her for wheelchair rides around the neighborhood on nice days, and often brought her home for visits with my father. I was instrumental in the replace-ment of a nurse who took it upon herself to cut down Mother's medication (because she was "too lethargic"), which resulted in a severe seizure, after which she could no longer walk at all.

Mother spoke to me once, for the first time in two years. She looked up at me and said "I'm sorry." A year later she died quietly in her sleep at the age of 81.

When Margaret faced the decision about a nursing home for her father, it was very different.

While Mother was in the nursing home, my father contin-ued to live with us. He was a sweet, easygoing man whom we all adored. But with the passage of time, the aging process began to take its toll.

First, he lost his balance. Through the Veteran's Administration we obtained a wheelchair. When I write the word "wheelchair" I find myself smiling, for we had many high adventures with this wonderful tool of mobility. I took my father everywhere with me. To Little League games, swimming lessons, Boy Scout outings, Christmas pageants at school. I would take him out into the garden while I worked there.

One day I asked him how he'd like to go on a boat ride. He shrugged his shoulders and wrinkled his nose. I said, "OK, let's go." We drove over the bridge to San Francisco and boarded the boat for Angel Island. I can still see his smiling face and his blanketed body braced against the wind on the uppermost deck where two muscular crewmen had so willingly offered to carry him, wheelchair and all. I pushed him on the trail that completely circled the island and we enjoyed the beautiful views. On the return trip the same two men were waiting to carry him back up for a repeat performance. I remember what a wonderful glow he had about him that evening at home.

Then we were suddenly faced with my father's incontinence. He was terribly embarrassed but I told him, "you cleaned me up once and now it's my turn." We laughed together as he said, "I always refused to do *that* job." Then he lost his ability to shave and wash himself. This meant "big kid" diapers (as my children called them) and my growing even more muscles to lift him in and out of the bathtub.

With time, my father became more and more quiet, often staring into his lap for long hours. He missed my mother. He forgot he was holding his cigarette and would burn his fingers or his clothes. From then on, I couldn't leave him alone. I remember with humor the day he looked at me and said, "Marg, I wish I could get on a motorcycle and hit the road!" I realized then how much he suffered by being so restrained.

I asked my father if he would like to visit the nearby Veterans Home, where he was entitled to live as a war veteran. I thought he might become motivated by some of the programs offered there. They had hobby classes, a movie theater, and lovely grounds where people could be outdoors. Many community activities were held there so special events were always available to the residents. I asked if he might be happier in the company of veterans of World War I like himself. He replied that he'd never thought of it but wouldn't mind giving it a try.

We went to visit and he offered to stay. I told him that if he was unhappy there, he could come home again. We settled on a one-month try. However, during the required initial medical examination, when he was asked to walk on his weak legs, he fell and broke his hip.

My father qualified for a small veteran's pension which, along with his Social Security, helped to pay for his stay there. I was able to keep money in his wallet for cigarettes or whatever he wanted to buy, so he did not feel destitute. He loved to pay for lunch when I took him out. I felt it helped him keep his dignity.

He stayed on at the veteran's home for the remaining years of his life, and I continued to visit him every week. We would go out to lunch and for long drives through the countryside. Once every month I brought him home for a few days, until the noise of the children and their friends made him nervous and he asked to go back. His sister later scolded me for "putting your very own father away."

Finding a good nursing home can be a challenge. Rinna, who worked full time, describes her search for a home for her father, who was living in another city when she began looking. He had been hospitalized for colon cancer, and his doctors advised him that he could not return home alone. The cost was not a major factor, since it could be covered by an inheritance Rinna's father had from his brother.

I searched for quarters that *felt* good. The key was getting a referral from the Social Service Department of an excellent local hospital. That gave me a place to start. I inspected ten local intermediate care facilities carefully. I soon learned what to look for. Spic and span was not essential. I sniffed for urine and other sour odors. I looked for rug stains, and at the equipment, furnishings, and general ambience. I observed the attitudes of aides, nurses, and the adminstration. How did they interact with the residents? Was physical therapy provided for all who could respond? Did the building feel filled with life and energy?

I returned to facilities I thought were a possibility, at lunch and dinner time. I wanted to see what was served and whether I would want to eat it too. Taking a day away from my job, I walked in on exercise and game programs. In some places all patients who were well enough were dressed and groomed. In others, residents lay dulled in bed.

If environment was important, so was safety. I checked the fire exits and looked for grab bars in appropriate places. I asked questions, especially about incontinence. Where Dad was finally placed, they clocked his habits and eventually controlled his toilet routine. Incontinence practically disappeared.

Once a relative is in a nursing home, caregiving still goes on. Visiting, monitoring the care, and supplementing it (if necessary) can still be very demanding.

Rinna was the only family member in the state, so all responsibility fell to her. She visited her father at the home five times a week. After the first month, she realized his dazed eyes, slow speech, and general inertia were caused by the medicine he was taking. She talked with his doctor and suggested he be taken off drugs. His improvement was slow, but "eventually, Dad made more sense. Today I realize that doctor was extraordinary because he respected *my* input," said Rinna.

Rinna worked out a program of exercises to supplement the 20 minutes of physical therapy her father received each day. She also took him on walks, pushing his wheelchair around the building. She brought large-size print books from the library and read to him, pausing to discuss a thought or phrase, or to connect the words to a moment in the past. "Once I brought a masseuse. Dad's eyes gleamed with pleasure as he received his first massage," she recalled. She taped his favorite songs, musical show tunes he used to sing around the piano with his wife. She sang along with the tape and he said it was wonderful.

Rinna and her father had not been close. "He had never approved of my life. But instead of holding onto grudges, I made our time together valuable," she said. As he grew stronger, she took him out for Sunday drives and to dinner at restaurants. "So what if his nose dripped and his food has to be cut? It gave him a few hours of freedom."

Often, our communication was through hugs and touch. I tried to bring laughter to the short time we still had together. Taking care of my father gave me an opportunity to express love, dispel grievances, and mend fences. After a lifetime of not being close, we shared warmth and a closer intimacy.

Still, Rinna felt lonely in her responsibility. In eleven months, her sister "called only three times and then it was to criticize."

My father's brother-in-law, who doled out funds for Dad's care, also criticized. No one was there at the end of the day for me to talk to, for comfort. No one offered to come and give me time off. No one ever told me I was doing a good job.

Rinna paid less attention to her career and her performance on the job suffered. Finally, as Rinna describes it, "I buckled." She became ill, and her father caught pneumonia and died soon after.

For Rinna, finding a good home and supplementing her father's care there was a difficult task, even though money was not a problem. However, far too few people find themselves in a situation like Rinna's, where adequate and acceptable nursing home care is available. In some areas of the country, there are simply not enough nursing homes to meet the need.

Cost can be a major factor. The choices are even more limited for people who cannot pay for their care: many homes will not accept Medicaid patients. Additionally, many nursing homes are reluctant to admit patients who require "total" or constant care and supervision.

Caregivers are often forced to send their relatives to nursing homes far away from where they live, making it difficult, if not impossible, for them to visit and monitor the care the patients receive. These problems make the necessary decision unnecessarily burdensome and ridden with anxiety.

Karen's story shows the financial pressures typically confronting most caregivers, and some of the anguish that comes when a good nursing home is not available.

Karen's mother, Clara, had Alzheimer's disease, and Karen had been taking care of her at home. Over the four years she cared for Clara, Karen had become progressively more exhausted, but she did not consider the possibility of infection, her doctor advised that she not go home again, and recommended that Karen place her in a nursing home.

Karen's own income was limited, and she certainly could not afford the $2,000 or more per month that good private facilities charged. Clara had minimum Social Security as her only income and was a Medicaid patient. The only nursing home that would accept a Medicaid patient was in another town, 30 minutes drive away.

Although Clara had been able to walk with a cane before entering the nursing home, on one of Karen's early visits she found Clara tied to a wheelchair. Clara had soiled herself, and when Karen asked the aides to give Clara a shower, they hastily washed her with vinegar and water. "She was still not clean. What she needed was sympathy, a shower and clean clothes from top to bottom," Karen recalled.

Clara stayed there eight months. Karen noticed there was a lot of turnover among the nursing staff, and few staff members seemed to have any training. Clara's dentures were lost, and her cane kept disappearing. If Karen hadn't come almost every day to take care of Clara, the time there would have been unbearable for them both. The family doctor knew of another facility that took Medicaid patients, and which was both better and closer to home. He kept inquiring for four months. "We were jubilant when a bed became available," said Karen.

The new home had better food and therapy treatments for Clara, but the nursing staff was still underpaid, inexperienced, and overworked. "The patients who had family nearby to fill in for the nurses did much better," Karen noted. Clara was happier at the new home. Karen continued to visit every day. She took home Clara's laundry and she brought Clara clothes and other things she needed that the nursing home did not provide.

Karen's story illustrates why many caregivers feel guilty and put off the nursing home decision as long as they possibly can. The fear that the care will be less than excellent, or clearly inadequate, is often a realistic one.

A caregiver may have to become an advocate for her relative at the nursing home, to make sure he or she gets good care. Yet many people rightly fear that if they complain too much about their relative's care, the nursing home may retaliate against the patient. If the patient is on Medicaid, options for a move to a better home may be limited, as they were for Clara.

In a number of ways, public policy makes the decision about a nursing home more difficult than it need be. Because services that would help a caregiver at home are rare and expensive, the choices are unnecessarily stark. It's either go on alone in an impossibly difficult situation, or find a nursing home. There's often no middle ground.

Thus, public policy sometimes dictates that caregivers opt for a nursing home sooner than they would like. For low-income caregivers, Medicaid regulations often make it easier to put someone in a nursing home than to get funds for any in-home services. In many areas of the country, home care and community-based services are hard to come by unless the caregiver is very wealthy. Many caregivers who would like to care for a relative at home are forced to consider a nursing home sooner because of lack of services.

Public policy can also mean that women keep caring for a relative at home long past the time when she would otherwise choose to. As we saw in Chapter 4, to avoid poverty, many middle-income wives care for their husbands at home longer than is good for their own health. For the woman who does not want to be a caregiver at all, the reputation of the nursing home industry and the reality of most nursing homes is often enough to persuade her otherwise. Good nursing home care does exist. However, it is such a low priority for America's social resources that many caregivers cannot expect their relatives will get it. This can deter any caregiver, even when good nursing home care would obviously be the best solution.

The decision about nursing home care will continue to be difficult until in-home services, respite services, day care centers, and high quality nursing home care are widely available, and a caregiver's personal finances are no longer the determining factor in whether she can get them. Until then, it will remain a decision fraught with guilt and anguish.

6

Complicating Factors:
Some Special Caregiving Situations

A number of situations can complicate the task of caregiving. Here, we will dicuss five of the more common ones. An increasing number of women are caregivers who also work outside the home. Caregivers with children at home face two generations with conflicting needs for nurturance. With adult children often living far away from their aging parents, more people find themselves caregivers at a distance. Minority caregivers, in general, face extra burdens. And there are some caregivers who are just not able, either psychologically or physically, to do the job.

The Employee Who Is Also a Caregiver

More and more people are living to older ages. Today, approximately 1 in 9 Americans is 65 or over, and by 2020, the ratio may be as low as 1 in 6. (The ratio in 1900 was 1 in 25.) Although most people at 65 are in good enough health to care for themselves, people in their 80s and 90s are much more likely to have disabling illnesses, and many more people are living to those ages.

At the same time, another trend is making the people who have traditionally cared for these older people less available. Their daughters and daughters-in-law are streaming into paid employment in record numbers. Fifty-one percent of working age women are in the labor force, and the number is rising every year. While many women in the present generation of caregivers did not grow up expecting to work throughout their lives, tomorrow's daughters and daughters-in-law are much more likely to have that expectation. What, then, are the burdens of paid employment combined with caregiving?

A Corporation Surveys Its Employees

The Travelers, one of the world's largest diversified insurance and financial services corporations, released what may possibly be the first study conducted by a corporation concerning the caregiving responsibilities of its full-time employees. The company surveyed a group of home office employees age 30 and older. It defined caregiving as "providing care for a relative or friend age 55 or older, who needed the employee's time or help because of illness or other limitations."

Not surprisingly, the results indicated that caregiving responsibilities differ markedly depending on the sex of the caregiver. Among Travelers' female employees, 63 percent reported that they were the primary caregiver, as compared to 29 percent of males, who reported relying more heavily on "outside help or their spouses" to provide the primary care.

The Travelers survey looked into the stress factor for their caregiving employees. It found that "coupled with the demands of a job and running one's own household, the additional responsibility of having to care for an older relative or friend can be quite stressful."

One question addressed whether caregiving responsibilities interfere with social and emotional needs and family responsibilities; the response indicated that only 2 in 10 caregivers did not feel any interference, 20 percent felt caregiving interfered frequently or most of the time, and 60 percent felt it did so sometimes. Among employees who indicated they were the primary caregiver (and these were mostly female) nearly 3 in 10 indicated that their caregiving interfered "frequently or most of the time."

Eighteen percent of those surveyed had not had a vacation away from those caregiving responsibilities for more than two years, and another 10 percent, for one year.

The study concludes, "In light of the demands caregiving can require, it is perhaps not surprising that, when asked whether caregivers felt that they could continue providing care for as long as necessary, 30 percent indicated they could but only with additional help, 20 percent weren't sure, and 5 percent felt they could not continue even with additional help."

A New Breed of Superwoman

The phenomenon of women attempting to compete with men on the job, while carrying on the complicated tasks of child-rearing, has been tagged "the superwoman complex." With the growing demand for yet another layer of caregiving, and with the average age of caregiving daughters only 50, a new breed of superwoman is in the making. This time, she is a combination of career woman and Florence Nightingale, with disabled adults, rather than children, the objects of care.

Myrna's mother, Esther, was diagnosed as having Alzheimer's disease. Esther lived alone; her husband had died three years before. Her son lived 3,000 miles away; Myrna was the only child in the area. Myrna taught English at a local junior college and was divorced. Her son, 15, and daughter, 10, lived with her.

When she heard the diagnosis, Myrna was stunned. How

could this happen to her lovely, bright, witty, loving mother? She vowed to care for her mother as well as her mother had cared for her.

Myrna started learning about Alzheimer's disease by reading books and talking to the doctors. She decided to keep her mother living in her own home as long as she could, to keep her comfortable in familiar surroundings. She knew she needed to hire help for her mother and to get her to a day care center. Then, things could be managed.

Esther knew she had a disease and that helped her understand why she felt something was terribly wrong. She knew she couldn't remember things well and sometimes she was terrified because she didn't know where she was. She was still driving, but she was careful to go only to the market and back.

When Myrna sent over a woman to help around the house, Esther was furious. This was her kitchen and she had never let anyone help her before. She liked to cook. She liked to do her own marketing. She liked to drive. When the worker came the second time, Esther wouldn't let her in. It was her home and she wasn't going to let anyone push her around—especially her daughter and a strange lady.

Myrna didn't know what to do. Her mother had always been a sweet person, but now she resembled her old self less and less each day—she wasn't bathing and the house was filthy. Myrna was afraid her mother would harm herself, or leave the burners on.

Myrna decided that if her mother wouldn't accept help from a stranger, maybe she'd accept help from her daughter. Also, maybe she could keep her mother from losing too much more of her memory. Maybe love could keep the Alzheimer's away. Every morning before work and every evening after work, she stopped by her mother's house. She bathed her, laid out her breakfast, and made sure there was food for lunch. After work, she fixed dinner for her and then went home to prepare dinner for herself and her children. On weekends, she cleaned her mother's house and did her shopping, as well as her own. Her kids helped. Her son called his grandmother when he got home from school to check on her and sometimes he did the morning routines with her.

Myrna tried sending her mother to a day care center, but her mother felt sick every time she was scheduled to go. She took the car away one day, telling her mother that it had gone to the shop for repairs. Her mother soon forgot.

Myrna's exhaustion increased steadily; finally she got the flu and a high fever. Her mother needed more and more help and Myrna couldn't be there. She called an agency and had a worker go out. Her mother didn't make a fuss; she let the worker help her. Myrna was relieved, but also very upset. Her mother no longer desperately needed her; others could help her now. All of her efforts had not stopped the deterioration. She felt she was now really losing her mother.

By now Esther was beginning to go out of the house and wander around the neighborhood. The neighbors would bring her home. Myrna hired 24-hour live-in care for her mother. It was very expensive, but her mother now liked someone with her, and it was necessary to make sure she was safe. To give the worker some free time and to provide more stimulation for her mother, Myrna sent Esther to the day care center three days a week. Esther adjusted well this time.

Myrna continued to grieve over her now childlike mother and to worry about the finances. Esther could afford ten more months of live-in help. After that, her assets would be gone. She appealed to her brother for help. He said he couldn't send money because it was all tied up. Myrna lived frugally, and with trepidation began looking at nursing homes.

In spite of around-the-clock supervision, Esther broke her hip six months later and moved into a nursing home. Myrna visited daily on her way home from work.

Limited Options

The choice to continue working or quit to become a full-time caregiver is not one regularly faced by men. For women, the choice is colored by such variables as financial need, attainment of career goals, and past family relationships. Whatever the outcome, the pressure is great and the options are limited.

One woman delayed her retirement because of her husband's illness:

My husband had a series of small strokes. Since he's been sick the last three years, he is in a wheelchair. He can't get up or down or anything by himself; he needs help. I have a nurse for him all day when I am working. When I go home at night, of course I take over. My job is sort of a release. I get there and put my husband completely out of my mind, and lose myself in my work.

I would have retired at 60 if it wasn't for my husband's condition. If we could be like we used to be, I would have left because I have worked so long. Forty years is a long time to work; after a while you get a little bit tired.

Also, my husband's condition is not getting better and probably never will. I can't afford to have the nurse eight hours a day if I am home, but I can't take care of him all by myself. I can't lift him. I can't bathe him. I'm just not a nurse. It makes me nervous, and I just can't manage him. I mean, you have to know how to hold people and do all sorts of things. She shows me a lot of things, she is wonderful, but it's something I just can't do.

Another woman found that retiring early was the only solution for her:

My father was still living, and he had been ill for about five years. It was just getting to be too much for me to work a full-time job and keep things covered here at home and see that he was taken care of, so I just felt that I'd be better off to stay home and take care of him. He lived for about eight months after I retired. I would still be working if I hadn't had that situation.

Other caregivers, like Carol (Chapter 2), must put their careers "on hold" for a time. The consequences to the caregiver may be lost pension credits or lost chances for advancement. As a report of the National Association of State Units on Aging states, "The role conflict among working/caregiving women is complex. The multiple roles assumed include employee, parent, spouse, filial caregiver and sometimes, grandparent. The combination of multiple role and value conflicts makes the working/caregiving woman a high risk health group."

Caring for Two Generations

The midlife caregiver is often thrust into a role for which she is unprepared. There is an unexpected shift in family organization and communication patterns. Relationships with her husband, children, and the older parent or other relative become complex.

A caregiver with children at home finds herself sandwiched between two generations. For her children, she needs to provide ongoing nurturing and guidance, an atmosphere in which they can grow, and the many small services that contribute to their being fed, clothed, groomed, and healthy. For her parent or relative, the midlife caregiver needs an expanded set of skills for an indeterminate period of time. These can include nursing, preparing special foods, giving financial assistance, and communicating with health care professionals and community service people. All of these services take on an added dimension of complexity and frustration when done on behalf of an elderly person who has lost his or her independence.

The decision to care for an aging parent at home should be made by an entire family, including young children. Everyone needs to see this as the family's responsibility rather than that of a single person.

Carol (whose story is told in Chapter 2) did not decide on her own that her father should move in with the family. Her husband was in on the decision, and the initial suggestion came from her teenage sons. "It was the boys' suggestion that we bring him home to live with us, because Dad liked being with us so much when we'd bring him home on weekends. So we took the plunge and brought him home," she said.

Children often have a helpful, unspoiled, and open kindness. Drawing children into a supportive role can be very beneficial to both the caregiver and the ailing parent. The children can develop a special relationship with the older person and age-appropriate responsibility can make them feel needed, mature, and part of the life of the family, while also giving the caregiver a break.

Carol's father began to have trouble understanding what she said to him. Parts of his brain were so badly damaged that even

simple conversations became trying. When he couldn't understand, he got frustrated and angry. He vented his anger on Carol.
And then Carol, in turn, would be impatient with her sons. "It
was very difficult for the boys to put up with me because I'd get
very stretched out. And so they would take over and call themselves the Senior Sitting Front, and they would stay with him
and send me off to do something else," she said.

Very young children can also be involved in caregiving.
They often have an imaginary world that meshes well with the
childlike behavior of an adult who has some form of brain
deterioration. They can sometimes maintain a loving and re-
laxed relationship with the older relative, free of the anxiety and
responsibility a primary caregiver feels. This type of involvement should be encouraged because it can help ease the burden
on a sandwiched caregiver.

But children can also come to resent the time and energy
their mother gives to an elderly person, and may demand the
attention they feel is rightfully theirs.

> Initially, Irene's mother had been a welcome addition to
> the household. She had helped occupy 7-year-old Heidi
> after school while Irene worked outside the home. The
> mother's stroke changed everything. Heidi had to go to a
> sitter after school, the grandmother attended an adult day
> care center, and now everyone arrived home at the same
> time, hungry for dinner. Irene began to feel overwhelmed
> by all the competing demands, especially those of her
> daughter, who felt deserted by both her mother and
> grandmother. Heidi became increasingly whiny and cling-
> ing, following Irene around from one room to another.
> Dinnertime was particularly chaotic. The last straw came
> when Heidi refused to eat dinner unless Mom spoonfed her
> the way she did Grandma.

Children in a caregiving situation may also experience depression, burnout, and resentment. They may not feel like they
have a close family anymore and as a result may misbehave or
spend less time at home than their parents would like. It is
important for a caregiver to discuss the matter with her children
and try to involve them in decision-making. Kids have a lot to
contribute, but at some point a disabled older relative in the
home may be too much for them.

This may be a factor in a caregiver's decision for a nursing
home (see Chapter 5). It may be good for the older person to be
cared for by the family, but is it good for the whole family?

The responsibility for two generations can be an enormous
burden on the "sandwich" generation.

Lena and Mac were raising two daughters, ages 7 and 9,
when they brought Lena's mother into their small apartment to care for her. Mac worked days as an unskilled
laborer; Lena worked from 3:00 to 11:00 as a hospital clerk.

For two years, Lena got up early to get the girls ready for
school. Her wheelchair-bound mother usually needed help
at the same time. A Medicaid-funded health aide came for
an hour a day and a companion for 6 hours a week, but
Lena's mother still needed a lot of her care.

The apartment was filled with tension. The girls disturbed
their grandmother with loud play and quarrels. Lena found
herself "yelling at everyone day and night." Mac became depressed, and Lena felt she "wasn't much of a wife to him."

Lena's mother took too many prescription drugs and began
having nighttime hallucinations. She would wake up
screaming at night and fall asleep during the day. Finally, a
case worker helped Lena choose a nursing home. Lena and
her mother cried the day her mother moved into the home,

but her mother gradually began to be happier there. She found a new social life and she was free of the constraints of her daughter's home. The staff monitored her medication and her health improved. Lena still brings her mother home on weekends and visits her during the week. She says they enjoy being together "a hundred times more" than they did when they all shared the small apartment. For this family, the nursing home was the best solution.

Two generations can stretch a caregiver to the limit. Often, a nursing home is the only choice because a "sandwiched" caregiver is trapped by the need for two services that are distinct non-priorities in America today: child care and home care for the elderly.

Giving Care at a Distance

Families in America today are geographically dispersed. When an older relative starts to need help, the first thought is usually that the relative should be moved to the caregiver's home or that the caregiver should move in and care for the relative.

But career responsibilities and family obligations can make either of these steps extremely difficult. Concerned family members can often be of assistance even if they live thousands of miles away.

Rinna (whose story of caring for her father is told in Chapter 5) had no warning before her mother was incapacitated by a sudden stroke. Rinna was a teacher in California; her parents lived in New York. Rinna's father managed to care for his wife for a while, even after she became incontinent. Rinna tried to be helpful over the phone, but her parents didn't want help. When she sent some special panties to help with the incontinence, though, her mother asked for more.

Rinna worried that her father was under too great a burden. One day, she stayed home from work and called long distance to agencies in New York that serve the elderly. One agency sent a caseworker out to talk to the couple, even though its normal procedure required that the request come from the person in need. The caseworker convinced Rinna's father to hire part-time help five days a week, to help with the care and do the cooking. "This kept Mother at home five years," said Rinna. Rinna visited during school holidays. Eventually, Rinna's mother had a second stroke and the doctors said she could not go home. Rinna flew to New York, helped her father find a good nursing home, and stayed two weeks, visiting her mother and monitoring her care. By the time she left, her mother had revived. She was able to sit up and have conversation.

A caregiver who lives far away from her relative may have some initial difficulty convincing the relative to accept outside help (as Rinna did). Even if she is able to do this, it is often hard to figure out where to begin. One good place is with the Area Agency on Aging in the older relative's community. This is a part of the local government and may be called Department of Aging, Social Service Department, or some other name. In the section on "Resources," a number of national organizations that assist caregivers are listed. These can be good sources of resources in the older relative's local area.

Minority Caregivers

When any woman in American today takes on the task of caring for an older relative, she faces a host of problems—emotional, physical, financial, and legal. But if she is also a member of a minority group, her task is likely to be more difficult still.

> Juana is only 29, but she's already been a caregiver for several years. Her father suffered from cancer and needed care for about a year before he died five years ago. Her mother had heart problems and couldn't do much of the heavy work involved in taking care of Juana's father, so she went to her mother's house every day to help care for him. Last year, Juana's mother became very ill. Juana brought her mother home with her and provided care during her mother's last four months. Now, Juana visits her grandmother every day and helps her with cleaning, cooking, cashing her Social Security check, and paying bills.
>
> Juana's husband, Ramon, drives a delivery truck and Juana works as a motel maid. They have two children, Teresa, 6, and Javier, 8. Ramon helps a little with the children and housework, but Juana's health has suffered because of her many responsibilities and the heavy physical work involved in caregiving and at the motel. She has severe muscle spasms in her back.

Juana's story is typical of some of the special circumstances that face minority caregivers.

A number of demographic trends converge to make minority group women more likely to be caregivers than white women. First of all, elderly members of minority groups are more likely to have held physically debilitating jobs, to have had limited access to health care, and to have lived in housing that was less than adequate. They tend, therefore, to have more chronic diseases and disabilities and to develop them at younger ages than their white counterparts. Second, a smaller percentage of elderly Hispanics and Blacks (than of whites) live in nursing homes.

Therefore, it appears that minority women are providing more care because their elderly relatives are more likely to need it and because their relatives are less likely to spend any portion of their lives in nursing homes.

Minority women are also more likely to come to the task of caregiving carrying additional burdens. Women in some minority groups—for example, Black women—are more likely than white women to hold jobs outside the home. They are more likely to face very long days when they combine caregiving with paid work and to have their livelihood threatened by the task of caregiving.

Minority group women are also more likely to be providing care to children, grandchildren, or other younger relatives at the same time they care for an older relative. This is true for two reasons. Because they get chronic illness earlier, older members of minority groups tend to need care at younger ages, at a time when their own children are more likely to still be parents of young children. Also, members of some minority groups are more likely to take on the task of raising grandchildren, nieces, nephews, and other young relatives during their own middle and later years.

Minority caregivers often face problems in two other specific areas: economic discrimination, and giving care in a cultural context that is not their own.

Economic Discrimination

Bernice is a 64-year-old Black woman who has been a domestic worker and waitress most of her life. Her wages have been low, and most of her employers have not paid into Social Security on her behalf. She's never had a job with a pension plan. She's taking care of her husband, Arthur, who at 67 has emphysema and arthritis.

Arthur has not been able to work for four years. Like

Bernice, his jobs have not always been covered by Social Security and were never covered by a pension. He gets a low Social Security benefit. Bernice would like to stop working herself, but she has no choice. The couple really needs her income. They have a daughter who lives in another state and is raising three children on her own, so she can't do a great deal to help, financially or otherwise.

While it would be a mistake to assume that all minority caregivers are poor, high rates of poverty among older members of minority groups—and especially older female members of minority groups—mean these caregivers are likely to have fewer economic resources than their white counterparts. Like Bernice and Arthur, they tend to arrive at retirement age without pensions and with minimal Social Security benefits.

A middle-aged minority caregiver is more likely to be in the labor force, where she is likely to be facing economic discrimination at work, with the result that she has less money to support her family. Facing triple discrimination—on the job, as an older woman, and as a member of a minority group — she shoulders the burden of caregiving while she is already loaded down with other problems.

Low income generally makes it harder to get services that might be of some help. Hiring someone to come into the home may be out of the question. Centers that provide services like respite care may be located far from minority neighborhoods, and transportation can be a problem. In some areas, services are available to the very poor through the In-Home Supportive Services program. However, with these and other services, the caregiver may encounter subtle or overt discrimination.

Low income generally goes hand-in-hand with limited educational opportunities. Many minority caregivers encounter difficulties with forms and letters and have problems communicating with highly-educated health care professionals when they have questions that need answers. Cut off from professional sources of support, the low-income minority caregiver is left to seek help from friends and relatives, even though resources are already thinly spread in low-income minority communities and families.

A Cultural Context That Is Not Her Own

Marian is a Black woman in her early 50s who cares for her mother while working full-time. She describes her experience trying to get some assistance:

> I don't ask for help. Once I did, and they gave me such a runaround at the county. "Call back after lunch" and "If you are working, you should be able to take care of these matters yourself." Finally when they did send a woman out, she was so disrespectful she left my mother in tears. I don't need that kind of help.

Marian is not the first minority caregiver who found that applying for publicly-funded services was demeaning and that the services were not helpful.

Health-care institutions, the Social Security and Medicare systems, nursing homes, and other services to caregivers are generally set up within the majority cultural context, creating problems for some minority caregivers. Language can be the biggest obstacle for Hispanic, Chinese, Japanese, and other non-English-speaking minorities. It can make many aspects of caregiving more difficult: getting clear information about an illness; applying for Social Security, Medicare, Medicaid, or other government benefits; taking advantage of services.

As the following story shows, sometimes language problems can be a matter of life and death.

Akiko, a Japanese-American woman, cared for her father, Hideo, during an illness two years ago. Today, Hideo is 90 and healthy. But then he was in a hospital on life-support apparatus and a respirator. Hideo was partially deaf and his limited English had deteriorated under the stress of illness.

The doctor misinterpreted Hideo's inability to communicate and told Akiko she had 24 hours to decide whether to stop the life support apparatus and respirator. "I went through such agony," she recalled. The next day, when the decision was to be made, she gave Hideo a pencil and paper and he wrote, "What time is it?" in Japanese characters. Akiko said, "That way, I could tell that his mind was functioning. I showed the paper to the doctor and he told me to forget about what he had said about stopping the respirator.

Language and cultural barriers can be a problem for whites, too, if they are immigrants.

Sophia and her husband came to America from the Soviet Union when they were 72 years old. Eight years later, he had Parkinson's disease and could not be left alone. Sophia cared for him at home, with the help of a worker from the Department of Social Services who came to her house nine hours per week. Sophia was disappointed that her daughter did not give her more help. In the old country, that would have been automatic.

After Sophia's husband was hospitalized with pneumonia, the doctors said he couldn't go home: he would have to go to a nursing home. The Jewish Home had a waiting list. The couple was on Medicaid and it was very hard to find a nursing home to take him. Finally, a home was found thirty miles away. He shared a room with two other men and the room smelled of wine. Sophia could see him only twice a week, once with her daughter on Sunday and once during the week when she took the bus—two hours each way. She cried every time she went. The nurses were nice, but they had too many people. Her husband couldn't tell them what he wanted. He spoke so softly now, and no one understood Russian or Yiddish.

After two months, he entered the Jewish Home. The communication problems were over, and the care was better.

For many minority caregivers, the ending is not as happy. The institution where a minority elder can be among his own people is not always available, affordable, or even in existence.

Minority caregivers find that the whole system of caring for the elderly is embedded in the context of the majority's values and customs. Few nursing homes serve Asian foods or encourage American Indian religious practices. Minority elders with low or no incomes are more likely to live in an extended family. If they do, they may be found ineligible for benefits and services, even though they would qualify if they lived alone.

Among Hispanics and other groups, some members of the household may be in the country without legal immigration papers. A caregiver may be reluctant to apply for any services or benefits, even if the older relative is a citizen and qualified to receive them. In combination, these factors mean that minority caregivers are even more likely than other caregivers to have to fend for themselves, without publicly-funded services and benefits.

When resources are available, minority caregivers come up with creative solutions. In one California community, a small group of Japanese caregivers formed a support group. They found a Japanese community agency willing to sponsor some houses run by Japanese workers, serving Japanese food. Their relatives stayed in these houses for short respite periods.

More often, support for minority caregivers comes from a strong, though informal, network of family and friends. In a minority neighborhood there is often a woman who is a key figure. She makes contacts with the larger bureaucratic world of social services, steers her neighbors in the right direction, and trouble-shoots when necessary. The divergence from the majority culture can also be a source of strength for minority caregivers; the cultural bond can give her access to informal help that has become rare in the relatively more modernized mainstream of America today.

Lesbian Caregivers

Older lesbians caring for their lovers with disabling illnesses face a different set of problems. Although the two women may perceive their living situation as a marriage, and it may have endured for decades, the law does not recognize it.

A lesbian caregiver may have great difficulty even getting information about her lover's condition from health care professionals. Some lesbians have been kept from their lover's hospital room when an insensitive hospital staff decided an illness was so acute that only "immediate family" should be allowed to visit. These problems can be avoided if the lovers formally give each other responsibility with a durable power of attorney for health care (see Chapter 4).

Lesbians may also face uncooperative blood relatives who do not acknowledge their love relationship or support their caregiving efforts. They may not feel welcome at support groups where other women discuss caring for husbands. It may be more difficult to apply for services for caregivers that are set up under the assumption that the person being cared for is a husband, parent, or sibling, and not a lifelong gay lover.

However, lesbians can call on special kinds of support. Many older lesbians have a network of supportive friends who help them when one becomes ill enough to need care. And as one lesbian caregiver, Marcy, discovered, gay health care personnel can sometimes help in unexpected ways:

> Lynne died of cancer five years ago. We had gone to the same doctor for maybe fifteen years before that, but we'd never thought too much about his personal life one way or the other. When Lynne had to go into the hospital, Dr. Taylor made sure I got to visit her whenever I wanted. I even slept over in the next bed several times. He treated me like a doctor would treat someone's husband or wife, even better maybe. Also, one of the nurses was very nice, very supportive. I don't think I could have gotten through it all without her. It was only later that I realized they gave me all this special attention because they were both gay, too.

Lesbian caregivers may be unable to get help from their own or their lover's relatives because the relatives disapprove of their sexual orientation. On the other hand, many older lesbians have networks of friends who help out when one in their group needs care.

Margaret describes being the coordinator between a group of friends and relatives and hospice:

> I kept track of the medications she was on, making out a sheet every week to show how much she should get when, so that people wouldn't double-dose her or forget to give her something. And every week I made a schedule of who was coming to help out, so that we always knew what the coverage was.

> Most of my time with Bobbi was spent helping her out

directly. I did whatever was needed, washing her, helping her to the commode or bedpan, trying to keep her comfortable and amused— real physical, practical, nuts-and-bolts things. Some of what I did wasn't really my role as it had been worked out, but all of us just did whatever was needed. We'd take calls from people wanting to visit and keep a visitors schedule so there wouldn't be an overload of people at one point and nobody at another. We were always answering the door as people sent flowers or dropped by.

When she was alive and well, her life was very open— people came in and out of it. It was like a house with all the windows open, and the wind and the elements just blew where they would, right through her. And in her dying days, in her house, it was very much like that, a continuation. People came and people went. They had free run— they came in, walked to the refrigerator, and helped themselves. People had access to her, and they had access to her dying and to her death, as well as to her living. That was a gift.

Lesbian couples who own a home together or have other joint property need good legal advice to find the best way to protect one partner financially if the other dies. In more than one case, relatives have taken property from a grieving lesbian lover who thought she co-owned it. If the agreement was strictly informal, she may not be able to stop it. Older lesbian couples need to make wills, especially if one is caring for the other.

Caregivers Who Are Not Able to Do the Job

Dorothy and Walter Healy had an agreement. Neither would ever send the other to a nursing home. Dorothy was twenty years Walter's junior and had also been a nurse.

Walter had several strokes, arteriosclerosis, emphysema, and severe hearing loss. Dorothy took entire responsibility for his care. She felt that as a former nurse, she knew what needed to be done, and that she ought to do it. She stayed with Walter all the time, always making sure he was comfortable. She would ask neighbors to watch him while she rushed off for an hour or so, to shop or go to Mass.

Then, Dorothy and Walter's oldest son, who was despondent over his job, committed suicide. Walter developed hives that itched so badly he scratched them until they bled. A doctor said they were related to stress caused by the son's death. Dorothy cried with frustration that she couldn't make the hives better. Walter was also having bad days; on one, he fell out of bed, and Dorothy, who was much smaller, struggled to put him back. Later that day, he mistook the living room for the bathroom, and had a bowel movement there.

It all became too much. At 71, Dorothy strangled her 92-year-old husband with a nylon stocking. The deputy coroner who investigated the murder called Dorothy Healy "a sweetheart—what everybody would like to have as a grandmother."

What happens when the caregiver herself can't really do the job because she is not up to it physically or psychologically, and yet is unable or unwilling to get help?

The newspapers speculated about Dorothy's "motive" for killing Walter. Did she want to end his misery, they asked, or did she snap under the exhaustion and strain of caring round-the-clock for her helpless, bedridden husband? Dorothy would not say; however, the two reasons are not as distinct as the papers made it sound. Dorothy found no avenue of help. She was determined not to break her vow and use a nursing home, and from the newspaper reports, even hiring help would have made her feel guilty. Her situation was extreme. But there are many caregivers who can't do an adequate job, and this can lead to their abusing or neglecting their relatives.

Very few caregivers intentionally harm their disabled older relatives. Caregivers who abuse or neglect their relative usually love them very much. They may not understand, or may deny, their own lack of ability. They may also be unable to find help. Services may be unavailable where they live, they may not know how to find services, they may not want to resort to the only service they know about—the nursing home. Like Dorothy, they may also be unwilling to accept help. This can be for many reasons: pride, a sense that only they can really do what is needed, or fear that the relative they care for will be taken from them if social service workers become familiar with the situation.

Jane and Nathan have been married for 55 years. He is 90, she is 83. They have no children and their closest relatives live 500 miles away. They have no close friends. They are proud of their independence and do not want help from social service agencies. Nathan has gradually lost interest in bathing and he is incontinent at times. He occasionally wanders away from home. Much to Jane's embarrassment, the neighbors bring him back. Jane is ashamed of his condition. It's getting harder and harder for her to bathe and change Nathan. She locks him in the house when she does the grocery shopping, a task she is finding more and more tiring. She's been having dizzy spells and has fallen down a few times. She forgets to turn burners off on the stove and has occasionally burned their dinner.

Jane and Nathan are in a dangerous situation. An accident that could harm either or both of them is a real possibility. As

Jane has more health problems herself, she may begin to neglect Nathan. Although Jane and Nathan don't want help, something may happen that is serious enough for a neighbor to call the authorities.

There are other types of precarious situations. One is with a caregiver who, throughout her life, hasn't even been able to take care of herself.

Adele is 78 and Rhonda, her daughter, is 43. Adele has taken care of Rhonda off and on throughout Rhonda's adult life. Rhonda has a history of violent behavior and drug and alcohol abuse and has been hospitalized for psychiatric care. When Rhonda comes home, Adele always gives her shelter and money. They've never gotten along very well, and their constant arguing makes it hard living together. However, Adele has always opened her home to Rhonda when Rhonda showed up at her door.

Now, Adele is needing care herself. She is losing her memory and is less and less able to cook and clean for herself and Rhonda. This makes Rhonda angry. She blames her mother and says, "She could cook if she wanted to, she's just trying to make it hard for me." Rhonda sometimes hits Adele. This upsets Adele, but she is afraid to be alone and wants her daughter with her.

When a caregiver, for whatever reason, can't perform the task, she puts her disabled relative, and possibly herself, in danger. With more people living longer with chronic illnesses, and nursing homes being so costly and often inadequate, dangerous situations at home will become more likely.

Elder abuse or neglect is often the outcome. Under increasing stress, caregivers may become physically violent in time of frustration, may not give medications when they are needed, or may not provide adequate food or personal care. Understanding and assistance are the solutions to the problem in most cases.

Often, services of the types we will describe in Chapter 7 can avert abuse before it happens.

Gene's Parkinson's disease came on gradually and he had little impairment for several years. As his wife, Paula, saw it, he had voluntarily stopped bathing and grooming himself during the fifth year of his illness. (Gene and Paula's story is told more fully in Chapter 2.) She felt he could be doing better and she didn't see it as her responsibility. Gene got worse. It got so that he was falling frequently and had minor injuries: bruises, bumps, and sores.

A visiting nurse saw Gene bruised, unwashed, and generally not well taken care of. She told Paula that if she didn't get some help into the home, Gene would have to go to a nursing home. Paula hired a home care worker to come in every day, but the cost was a financial strain. She didn't want to put Gene in a nursing home, though, because that would completely drain the couple's savings. At 68, Paula managed to find a part-time job and now works half a day while the home care worker cares for Gene.

In situations more serious than Paula's, like those of Adele and Rhonda or Jane and Nathan, ongoing supervision by a case manager is necessary. A case manager is a social worker or registered nurse who assists a family member—making decisions, locating and arranging for services, and supporting the caregiver. Unfortunately, case management services are far from universally available.

In extreme cases, especially in areas where case management is not available, an older person who is being abused and neglected may be involuntarily separated from the caregiver. This generally means entry into a nursing home, something the older person may dread more than staying in a home where abuse or neglect occurs. If the person refuses, sometimes a court proceeding will force the matter.

Support services for caregivers that are readily available and affordable could avert some of these tragic situations by solving the problem before it becomes so extreme.

Many states have recently adopted laws about elder abuse. Most of these laws require any professional who has knowledge of abuse of an older person to report it, usually to the Department of Social Services. However, these laws don't always require that someone investigate the situation or help the abused elder or caregiver. While mandatory reporting laws are a necessary first step, they are inadequate without support services for both the abused elder and the caregiver.

To the extent that our nation leaves the care of chronically ill older people entirely up to family caregivers, the country is gambling with the welfare of its older people. Many older people will be lucky to have a caregiver who can cope on her or his own. Others will not be so lucky. Under present conditions, help often comes too late or not at all for caregivers who aren't able to do the job. A society that assumes a partnership with family caregivers for the welfare of its older citizens can provide services in time, before abuse is likely to occur.

7

Getting Some Help:

Services for Caregivers

Services to caregivers are of two types. The first type provides someone else to do the actual care, which may be in the home, at an adult day care center, or at a residential facility. The second type helps the caregiver to cope better. Self-help groups and counseling don't make the caregiver's work week any shorter, but they can help her organize and face that week a little more easily. These services can substantially lift the burden of caregiving. However, they are not always available or affordable, and just finding them can take an enormous effort.

Too often, caregivers are reluctant to seek services, even when they are available and affordable. Many caregivers do not know that service even exists. Some feel they should be able to solve their problems on their own, without turning to outside help. Some feel guilty for wanting to get away from caregiving. Some are uncomfortable with a stranger coming into their homes. Some feel that no one can care for their relatives as well as they can.

The fact is, caregivers really need all the help they can get. Support services can be preventive measures. The stress of caregiving can lead to emotional and physical breakdown. When this happens, everyone—the patient, the caregiver, other members of the family—suffers. Waiting until a crisis erupts before looking for services means that the choices will probably be more limited and the stress on both patient and caregiver will be greater. Not all the services described in this chapter are available in every community. Some may be available, but too costly. Not all types of services are appropriate to the needs of every caregiver. But it is well worth the time and effort it takes to find out what services are available, and to try them out to find the services that can be most helpful. The result can be better health for both the disabled older person and the caregiver.

Finding services may take some time and ingenuity. A good place to start is with local Senior Information and Referral phone lines. These are often located at senior centers, or the workers at a senior center may know where to find the nearest one. Another source of information is state or local departments of aging or social services (see "Resources," for details on how to find these). Another good place to begin is with a social service worker at a reputable hospital.

Home Care

There are several advantages to having someone come into the home to provide care. Remaining at home is least disruptive for the patient, especially if he or she is very ill or confused. The usual routine can be maintained and the hours can be flexible. However, home care is usually the most expensive alternative, it can be less stimulating for the patient, and it can be time consuming for the caregiver to set up.

Home care may be provided by professionals, such as nurses, physical therapists, speech therapists, or occupational therapists. For most families, the amount of care a patient can receive from a professional is limited by what Medicare, Medicaid, or private insurance will pay.

Most often, home care by a professional is initiated as part of a discharge plan when a patient leaves a hospital after an acute illness. If the patient is unable to get out of the home to use rehabilitation services, a physical, occupational, or speech therapist may make a limited number of home visits. If the patient needs a skilled nurse for services such as injections or dressing changes, a registered nurse or licensed vocational nurse may come to the home. Once insurance, Medicare, or Medicaid coverage for these visits runs out, the expensive visits are discontinued. The professionals can often teach the caregiver useful skills and answer questions that will help the caregiver cope on her own.

Most care in the home does not require sophisticated medical skills. Most can be done by home health aides, homemakers, or attendants. The purpose is usually to give the caregiver some respite. The worker needs to be knowledgeable about the disability, have emergency care skills, and be sensitive to the needs of the caregiver and patient.

Home care attendants may be hired to provide the caregiver a few hours respite each week. They may come every day, even providing care while the caregiver works at paid employment. The most expensive arrangement is to hire a full-time live-in attendant. These people receive room and board with a substantial salary; the caregiver must still expect to cover regular days off each week.

Finding a good home care attendant, as many a caregiver has learned, can be a formidable challenge. This person will almost become part of the extended family and will know things about the patient and caregiver that not even friends see. For many caregivers, this is the first experience in hiring someone.

One place to start is a registry. Hospitals and social service agencies (such as Jewish Family and Children's Services or Catholic Social Services) sometimes maintain lists of home care workers. Usually, the applicants haven't been screened. The caregiver must check on the person's experience and references herself. An advantage of using this method is that it is flexible; the

133

caregiver can set the terms of employment, including the attend-ant's wages.

The disadvantage is that the caregiver becomes an employer. She must keep records, deduct payroll and Social Security taxes and forward them to the government, along with other respon-sibilities. Sometimes it is possible to make an arrangement for the home care worker to work as an "independent contractor," where he or she agrees to take responsibility for taxes. If there is no agreement about this in writing, the caregiver may later be held liable for back taxes.

Besides the arrangement for taxes, a written contract with the attendant can save a lot of potential trouble and heartache for the caregiver. The contract should spell out what services the work-er is expected to perform, as well as terms of payment. General-ly, if the patient requires heavy care, attendants will not do any household chores. If the patient requires supervision and lighter care, the attendant may do some chores such as preparing meals and doing dishes or laundry. Many problems between caregivers and attendants arise over what the attendant's duties should be. A written agreement from the beginning can help avert a problem.

Another way to recruit an attendant is through a home health agency. They are found in almost every community and are list-ed in the yellow pages of the telephone book. In addition to home care attendants, they supply physical, speech and occupational therapists, medical social workers, and people who will help with household chores. The advantage of using an agency is that they take care of the employment arrangements. They pay employee taxes and other benefits and schedule their employees. They are responsible for the quality of workers and can help in locating other community services. The disadvantage is that they are usually more expensive because the agency keeps a portion of the fee it collects from the caregiver.

Home care attendants can also be recruited by placing a want ad, going through the state employment agency, through a local church, or by word of mouth. These methods carry greater risk of turning out to be the caregiver's worse nightmare (although recruiting through agencies can sometimes carry risk, too). Many caregivers tell horror stories of hiring someone who later turned out to have a long criminal record or who only stayed on the job long enough to empty the family liquor cabinet. A caregiver should carefully check the references of any person she plans to bring into her home.

No matter how the attendant is recruited, a caregiver should plan on staying home for the first few visits. Not only will the patient have a chance to get used to the new situation, the caregiver can give training about the patient's special needs, observe how the attendant interacts with the patient, monitor the care, and decide if the attendant will work out.

Many caregivers have unrealistically high expectations of home care workers. They expect them to be a combination of a skilled nurse and a personal maid, or to duplicate the sensitivity to the patient's needs that the caregiver developed over years. Many caregivers find they can never expect an attendant to do as well as they can. Others, however, say that an attendant can be more objective or more skilled and actually do better. Home care is probably the situation where the personalities of caregiver, patient, and attendant play the most significant role in success or failure of the arrangement.

Paying for Care

Most home care is paid for privately, out of the caregiver's pocket. Medicare, Medicaid, and private insurance may provide some limited coverage. Medicare typically provides only a few visits from skilled professionals in a few types of medical situations. Medicaid may do the same; low income patients may in addition be eligible for a wide variety of home care (In-Home Supportive Services) if they meet certain criteria that vary by state. Some private insurance policies pay for more nursing care at home than Medicare allows.

A few communities have special programs that provide home

care for a sliding-scale fee. Some social service agencies (such as Lutheran Social Services, Jewish Family Services) also provide home care on a sliding scale. If the patient is in the terminal phase of cancer, some home care may be available through a hospice program, and Medicare may pay for hospice services.

Some communities have volunteer respite care programs, providing free care from a trained volunteer. The amount of time is usually only a few hours per week, but occasionally the volunteers are willing to take over while the caregiver is on vacation. These programs are generally sponsored by churches, government agencies, or volunteer organizations.

Adult Day Care

Although there are 1,000 adult day care centers in the U.S. today, the service is far from universally available. Where it is available, it can be an affordable means of respite for the caregiver and a stimulating experience for the client.

The most common type of program is called an *adult social day center*. At a typical program, transportation will be provided for the client, door-to-door, in a van. Clients arrive around 10:00 A.M. There is a morning get-together with staff to go over the day's schedule, greet each other, and talk about why someone may be absent. Some sort of activity (such as an adult education class, arts and crafts, cooking, exercise adapted to disabilities) follows. Clients who don't want to take part might read by themselves.

Lunch is generally a hot meal provided by the center, followed by a quiet period for rest. Many centers have recliners or cots for those who need them. Activities similar to the morning program follow, and clients are taken home around 3:30.

At an *adult day health center*, the day's program is similar. But in the course of the day, clients will leave the group for speech, physical, or occupational therapy; for counseling with a social worker; for treatment by a nurse; or for a visit with a podiatrist.

There are many variations in adult day care programs. Some are open only two days a week. Others will let a client come early and stay late, every day, to assist a caregiver who works full-time. Some programs exclude people who are incontinent, have Alzheimer's, or are in wheelchairs; other centers have been set up especially to handle these very clients. Many centers will take a client who falls outside their usual criteria on a trial basis.

While many centers provide transportation, a caregiver who lives outside a specified geographic area may have to take her relative to the center herself. Getting the person she cares for ready to go can also be a lot of work. In general, day care centers are not appropriate for anyone who is completely bedbound.

Adult day care is a new service and most centers are small, ranging from 5 to 50 clients. There is usually only one center per geographic area, but because the service is new there may not be a waiting list. The center may be flexible and tailor care to suit the individual. A disabled relative may not want to go to a center at first, but it is wise to try at least three times, to give the person a chance to get used to the new situation.

Paying for Care

Many adult day care centers have sliding scale fees; some run on donations only. In some states, Medicaid will pay for adult day care for a person who is financially eligible. A few private health insurance policies reimburse adult day health care. Since most adult day care centers are non-profit enterprises with funding from government, church, foundation, or charity sources, the care will usually be less expensive than home care.

Overnight, Weekend, and Vacation Respite

Some home health agencies will supply people for an overnight or weekend period of respite care. An arrangement of this type can be expensive; usually the caregiver must pay for three 8-hour shifts and a weekend could cost $500.

A few nursing homes have started offering short-term admissions. Because of the paperwork involved, and because of the difficulty the disabled relative will probably have adjusting to the situation, this is not a good option for an overnight or weekend. It may, however, be worth considering for a vacation of a week or longer. A two-week stay may cost $600 - $1,000 or more, especially if the person has Alzheimer's. In most cases, the caregiver must bear the cost of short-term nursing home stays.

A Story of One Caregiver's Use of Services

John had a very bad stroke seventeen years ago. He spent three months in the hospital, then three in a convalescent hospital. Then his wife, Nell, was told that Medicare would not cover any more; she should take him home. John's right side was paralyzed. A neurologist told Nell that John would never speak again, but she was determined to try. Under Medicare, a speech therapist came to work with John in their home 3 times a week for six months. A physical therapist also came, "and that was really helpful," Nell recalled. "She taught me easier ways to do a lot of things."

Nell found these professionals through the Easter Seal Society, which had a referral service. The home therapy only lasted six months; but the Easter Seal Society organized a weekly speech therapy class that met for 2 hours at a church. Nell took John for three years; he made no progress "but he really loved it."

Next, Nell enrolled John in a weekly speech stimulation group with twenty other people who had had strokes. "That was wonderful for him," she said.

The class and the group weren't designed to give Nell a

break, however. So when she had to go shopping, she would leave John alone, tying his paralyzed leg to his wheelchair. "I had to do that, because one time it went into spasm and he fell out and broke his hip. But I knew it wasn't right." She would shop or do her errands "in a frenzy" and hurry back to John.

She began looking for someone who could stay with John while she was out. She contacted a private agency. The first person they sent was a registered nurse. "But I think she had had some kind of a nervous breakdown," said Nell. "She was a nonstop talker, and I found it hard to get out of the house. She said she wouldn't come more often than one afternoon a week because it was too hard to take care of him. But all she did was give him coffee and then she just sat there and crocheted. The agency did not really screen these people very well. Another woman they sent was helping him use the bathroom and she let him fall. She had to call the police to get him back in his wheelchair."

Nell had a friend who was a physical therapist. She came sometimes to stay with John, as did other friends. Nell paid her friends the same wage she had paid the nurse from the agency. Still, this help was sporadic; friends only came in once a month.

After eight years, an adult day care center opened in Nell's community. A social worker approached Nell and two other women whose husbands had strokes, and the three men became the day care center's first three clients.

"I was reluctant to try the day care center. I was falling apart. I'd had about all I could handle. It was hard to get him into the car in his wheelchair and take him there. But for his sake, I tried it." Nell stayed with John at the center most of those first times.

The social worker encouraged Nell to let a van pick him up and bring him home from the center. "I had such a time, then, getting him to go. He didn't understand. I was worried they wouldn't be able to figure out when he needed to go to the bathroom. We were both crying the first day he left. Those first two weeks, he just glared at me when the van came. He wouldn't even wave goodbye.

"But after two weeks, things changed. The care at the center was good. John got a good lunch and the staff was able to handle the problem of the bathroom. He wasn't unhappy there anymore. I'd go over there at lunch time, and John didn't seem to care if I was there or not."

The stress of caring for John had given Nell a bad back and other health problems. As her health got worse, she increased John's time at the adult day care center to 3 days a week, from about 9:30 to 3:30.

John had retired at 65 with no pension; the couple lived on Social Security in a home that was paid for. The day care center had a sliding fee scale that made John's care affordable.

After three years, though, Nell's back got worse. She had to take painkillers all the time. The social worker at the adult day care center told Nell that if John didn't go to a nursing home, Nell might get so ill she could no longer care for him. The family doctor agreed. "He said if I didn't put John in a convalescent home, I'd have to go into one myself."

The social worker helped Nell get Medicaid benefits for John, since the couple could not afford the cost of nursing home care. But no nursing home in the area wanted to take John. "They didn't want any more hard-care patients," said Nell. John weighed over 200 pounds and needed assistance and a hydraulic lift for moving between bed and wheelchair. The only word he could say was "no."

Finally, the social worker from the adult day care center called one of the homes and they agreed to take John. Nell goes every day at noon and cares for him until 4. His sister then arrives and stays several more hours. "We do everything. We lift him, change his clothes, dress his bedsores, bathe him. From the moment we come in, the staff there doesn't have to go near him," she said.

Self-Help Support Groups

Support groups bring caregivers together to share feelings, exchange experiences, and learn from each other. They differ from traditional group therapy in that the purpose is not to change the members' behavior but to help them make decisions and cope effectively. Many self-help groups are led by a caregiver. Some use professionals as resources, either to facilitate the meetings or to provide information.

Most support groups allow new members to join at any time. They meet monthly, weekly, or twice a month. Some groups have dues to cover mailings and materials; many are free. Some groups may be time-limited with a specific focus, such as a series of educational workshops.

Support groups can provide many benefits:

Recognition. Too often, relatives and friends don't appreciate the hardships of caregiving, or a caregiver may not want to burden them with her complaints. A support group is a roomful of people who appreciate how much time, effort, and skill the caregiver gives to her task.

Empathy. A support group can be an outlet for talking about problems that no one else understands. It can be a safe, non-threatening environment where a caregiver can discover that many other caregivers share her reactions and feelings.

Social contact. Caregiving can be very isolating. A support group provides new contacts, friendships, and, in some cases, opportunities to share care responsibilities.

Education. Many caregivers are extraordinarily ingenious when it comes to devising solutions to their problems. A support group can be seen as a gathering of "experts" where those who face the problems share their creative solutions. Members often share a wealth of information about community resources and medical problems. Outside professionals may also be invited as guest speakers. Many caregivers need practical information, and support groups are an effective and inexpensive way to get it.

Advocacy. When a group of caregivers see a need, their combined voices speak more loudly than one voice alone. Many support groups have been the catalyst for starting respite programs, day care centers, volunteer in-home care services, and other much-needed community services.

Some groups have testified before state and local government bodies about the problems they face. Some have had legislation introduced or have lobbied for legislation favorable to their cause. For example, Alzheimer's Disease and Related Disorders Association, a national network of support groups for the families of people with Alzheimer's disease, successfully lobbied for more federal research funds to study the cause and search for a cure for the disease.

Caregiver groups have become teachers to both the general public and health care professionals. Some have become part of the curriculum in hospitals, clinics, and universities. Others have publicized their cause in the media. Because caregivers deal daily with the practical problems, they become the best teachers. They also know which solutions will work.

Says Barbara Deane, who started a group in Concord, California: "It's been very therapeutic to realize you're not alone with a problem. For example, I thought that my mother's bad relationship with her grandson was unique, but I learned that it's very common for elderly people to compete with their own grandchildren for the caregiver's attention. The elderly have as many special needs as children. We have had access to a lot of parenting education but very little geriatric education. A very important addition to our team has been a geriatric RN who came to the first meeting to observe, but has been an indispensible source of information and strength."

Says another caregiver: "The support group is very helpful. It gives me a chance to vent my own frustration and I get a lot of good feedback that helps me cope with what I'm up against. I realize I'm not alone and there are other people who have the same problems."

The National Support Center for Families of the Aging has a set of "affirmations" for support groups (see next page). These sum up the philosophy of a good support group.

Finding a Support Group

You may get help finding a nearby support group through your local Senior Information and Referral office, mental health clinic, Department of Aging or Social Services, a hospital, or a physician. Many national organizations will give referrals to local support groups. A list of them can be found at the end of the book, in "Resources."

Counseling

Individual counseling, family counseling, and case management can be valuable to caregivers in need of support and direction.

Individual counseling can provide a safe environment to explore feelings of anxiety or depression. It can help caregivers who feel overwhelmed and hopeless. A trained professional can identify the causes of feelings of burden and distress, and may help find solutions that have previously eluded the caregiver. Counselors can also find services and explore fears or hesitations the caregiver may have about using them.

Affirmations of the National Support Center
for Families of the Aging

1. We accept each other without judgment and are willing to offer and receive mutual caring and support in total confidentiality.
2. We are receptive to new skills and insights.
3. We are open to learning new ways of relating to the elderly.
4. We expect change as part of life; people can learn to understand and handle change.
5. We realize that we cannot control all the circumstances of our lives, nor of our loved ones' lives; we can work on our own reactions to them.
6. We believe that each person in our family—including ourselves—is entitled to a fair share of our time and resources.
7. We help each other consider alternatives, acknowledging that we can be more loving to our aging relatives when we are comfortable with our level of involvement in their care.
8. We summon courage to look at the reasons for any compulsive behavior that is giving us trouble; we do not base our decisions on the approval of others.
9. We admit that we cannot produce happiness for anyone else, including our aging loved ones; nor can we expect to fill all their needs.
10. We strive to clarify what is important to us and to consider any decisions on the basis of our true values, recognizing that any decision involves a cost.
11. We search for meaning in our experiences and seek to appreciate the benefits of knowing our relatives in their old age.

Ellen was very depressed. She had been caring for her 75-year-old husband, Henry, for four years. He had Parkinson's disease and he was getting worse. Ellen found she was no longer able to leave him alone to run errands because he might fall. She felt tired all the time.

She felt that her life was now hopeless, with nothing to look forward to but Henry's death and her own eventual illness and death. She and Henry had never been very social; they had kept to themselves and enjoyed a stimulating, loving relationship together. That closeness was gone; he was confused at times and very withdrawn. She was alone with him most of the time. Although she did speak regularly on the phone to her two daughters, they didn't live close by. Both were deeply concerned with their parents' situation.

Ellen's daughter Sandy suggested that she seek help. Sandy contacted a local community mental health center that had a special geriatric counseling department. Ellen was hesitant at first about going there. She had never talked to anyone but her close family about her personal life, and she was afraid and embarrassed to reveal herself. She also didn't want to spend money to talk to someone when she could talk to her daughters for free. In the end, Sandy's insistence and Ellen's own desire to feel better won out, and she contacted the social worker.

Ellen began meeting with the social worker on a weekly basis. She hired help to stay with Henry while she was gone. With the help of the social worker, she began to understand why she was feeling so depressed. She wasn't crazy, she was reacting normally to an overwhelming situation. She needed a safe place to fully grieve for her lost life. The counselor's office became that place. In time, Ellen began to focus on small pleasures that could relieve the constant stress of caregiving. She hired more help and began to swim again regularly. She discussed the guilt she felt about leaving Henry alone but came to realize that unless she took care of herself, she couldn't take care of him.

After about three months of counseling, she brought up the dreaded, most painful subject—putting Henry in a nursing home. Her daughters were telling her that it was time; Henry was falling more and more and he was beginning to hallucinate. He had hit Ellen a few times during these periods. She knew that getting more help wasn't the answer, since attendants probably couldn't handle him if he had violent outbursts.

She decided to wait and see if the situation would get better. It didn't. With the help and support of her social worker, physician, and daughters, Ellen began to look at nursing homes. It was difficult to find a home that would take Henry because of his violent outbursts. A local home, however, was just starting a special unit for people with Alzheimer's disease. Even though Henry had Parkinson's, they accepted him because his behavior indicated that he probably also had Alzheimer's.

Ellen continued to see her social worker regularly. She needed a safe place to work through her guilt about putting Henry in a nursing home, her sadness about visiting him, her loneliness, and her fears concerning her future.

Family counseling can also be very helpful. The stresses of caregiving, differing expectations of family members, and communication problems can increase anxiety and tension in a family.

The crisis generated by an elder's disability requires that a family come together in a new way. The family may need to decide who should assume the new responsibilities, such as management of home care workers and finances. They may also need to make decisions about a nursing home. These difficult decisions and tasks require flexibility, adaptability, and good communication.

Many families are unable to reach decisions or may deny some aspects of the problem. One child (usually the daughter) or the wife may be assuming most of the responsibility without support from other family members and may become resentful and angry. Family counseling can help each member understand the problem from the others' perspective and help the family formulate a plan that works.

Deborah knew that her husband's family needed help to manage her mother-in-law, Lillian. Lillian's husband, Sam, had died of a sudden heart attack two months before. He had cared for Lillian, whom they all had thought was just a little forgetful. After Sam's death, however, they realized that Lillian couldn't cook or shop for herself and needed help bathing and taking her pills. When Deborah spoke to Lillian's doctor, she found out that Sam had known that she had Alzheimer's, but hadn't told anyone else in the family.

Lillian had two other sons in the area. Both were married, but Deborah was the only daughter-in-law who wasn't working. Deborah knew that arrangements and plans had to be made for Lillian's care, but she didn't want to do it all alone.

Deborah contacted Jewish Family and Children's Services in her area and asked how to begin. She spoke with a geriatric social worker who recommended books and articles on Alzheimer's disease. Then she scheduled a family meeting of all three sons and their wives. At the meeting, major issues of concern were identified: Lillian's day-to-day care, financial management, handling Lillian's grief over her husband's death and her unhappiness over changes in her life, and future planning for her care.

147

The brothers were not used to being responsible for their mother. It was new and overwhelming for them, and they didn't yet understand the downward course of Alzheimer's disease. They also were still grieving for their father.

The other daughters-in-law were concerned for Lillian, wanted to be helpful, but were clear that they did not want to assume caregiving responsibility for her. The brothers had never been very close to each other. While they wanted to help their mother, they needed assistance in talking with each other and deciding who would do what.

The family met with the social worker for three planning and education meetings and then on an unscheduled basis, as needed, during the course of Lillian's illness. They also called the social worker from time to time. With the social worker's help, the family arranged for home care for Lillian and placement in a board and care home when she needed more supervision. The brothers and their wives decided among themselves who would take responsibility for her finances and who would help her adjust to the moves. They had arguments and much sadness, but in the end this painful process brought the family much closer together. The family felt that having a knowledgeable social worker whom they trusted was invaluable.

A *case manager* is a type of counselor who helps a caregiver find and get services. A case manager will look at the needs of both the patient and caregiver, make recommendations, and help set up the services. Case managers can be especially helpful to caregivers who themselves have some level of disability.

Anna called Catholic Social Services to see if she could hire an attendant from their home care brokerage program.

Her husband, Ralph, had had a severe stroke the year before and she had recently taken him out of a nursing home because she wanted to care for him at home.

Ralph was bed-bound, paralyzed, and unable to speak clearly. He was 89 and Anna was 82. They had no children and no close family in the area. A Catholic Social Services social worker visited them to see if other services were needed. She found that although Anna desperately wanted her husband at home, she was not even able to turn him over because of her arthritic hands.

Anna was also extremely depressed about her situation, cried frequently, and showed impaired judgment and slight memory loss at times. She knew she needed help with Ralph, but her savings were dwindling, and she couldn't afford to hire help for the full number of hours she needed it.

The social worker, after assessing the situation, felt that ongoing case management was needed to ensure that the couple utilized services appropriately and were both safe in the house. During the subsequent two years that Ralph remained at home, the social worker visited at least monthly and more frequently when necessary. She arranged doctor appointments and transportation, introduced new home care workers to Anna, helped her pay bills, and gave supportive counseling when Anna was feeling particularly depressed. She also provided access to some government programs that helped Anna pay for care.

Finding a Counselor

All three types of counseling described above can be found through family service agencies, community mental health centers, specially trained private practitioners, and special programs that have been set up to provide counseling.

149

It is important to find a counselor who has special training and knowledge about working with older adults and their families. As a consumer, you have a right to ask if the counselor has specialized geriatric training or experience working with older clients.

To decide whether a counselor is right for you, check up on his or her qualifications. Use your own intuitive judgment to decide if you feel comfortable, listened to, and respected. Does this counselor seem able to help find solutions that are right for you? Does the counselor have information you need about community resources? You may need to try several counselors before you find the right one.

Paying for Counseling

Many social services agencies and community mental health agencies have sliding scale fees. Services may be available free of charge or at a fee based on the family income. Medicare will pay for a limited amount of outpatient psychotherapy, but it has to be under the direction of an expensive psychiatrist.

Some communities fund case management programs. When these are funded through Medicaid, the disabled older person must meet poverty criteria to qualify. The programs include counseling, and are available to older people who might have to go to a nursing home without the services. Case management, counseling, and other services are available through these programs at minimal or no cost.

Respite care, hospice services, support groups, and counseling can all help ease the burden of caregiving. Too often, though, these services are not available or affordable. For this reason, too many caregivers still have to go it alone. Society is still a long way from undertaking a partnership with caregivers that would guarantee the welfare of our nation's chronically ill elderly. Next, we turn to reforms—the steps in making such a partnership a reality.

8

Making Changes:
Reforms Needed Today, Longer-Term
Solutions, and How to Get There

When someone you love spends years chronically ill, slowly declining, and finally dies, it's a difficult experience under any conditions. But the social conditions within which today's caregivers work make it far more difficult than it need be. It's time for society to acknowledge that each of us may face chronic illness in old age and that each of us may need care. Caregiving is socially necessary work, and society should acknowledge this by entering into a partnership with caregivers to see that the job is done well.

As we have shown in preceding chapters, America is far from being in partnership with its caregivers. Caregivers are mostly left to fend for themselves until (and sometimes even after) they reach their emotional, financial, and physical limits.

In this chapter, we describe some legislative reforms that can take our society several steps toward the goal of a partnership with its caregivers and some more comprehensive solutions to fully establish that partnership. We also describe how to win these reforms—by building a caregivers' movement.

Reforms Needed Today

This is an era of cost-cutting in government. So it is tempting to argue that the reforms we propose may save the government money. In many cases, this will be true, as in the following three examples.

1. As things stand today, a middle-class woman may start out caring for her husband with substantial assets and adequate income. His illness may leave her in poverty, dependent on the government for welfare for the rest of her days. Protecting at least a portion of her assets and income will mean that the government pays more for her husband's care in the short run, but less for supporting her in the long run.

2. Similarly, services that ease the physical burdens on caregivers may prevent the caregivers themselves from becoming disabled, thereby saving money for various government programs such as Social Security Disability, Medicare or Medicaid.

3. A caregiver who has the help she needs may choose to keep her relative at home and out of a nursing home, ultimately saving both the federal government and her state government thousands of dollars in Medicaid payments to the nursing home.

The reforms we outline in this chapter will not be cost-effective in all cases. This can only be expected, since in most cases society now does nothing to help caregivers. Doing something is going to cost more than doing nothing.

The way things are today, the only help a caregiver can count on is help in paying for nursing home care after she has exhausted and impoverished herself. The choice is too stark. If she has options for help along the way, she will probably use some of them earlier in the course of her relative's illness, with the result that caregiving will be a less catastrophic experience for her and her relative will get better care. On the whole, it's going to cost society something. Most caregivers are already making an enormous sacrifice. It's time for society to acknowledge that and to shoulder some of the burdens.

The reforms we describe here necessarily take a piecemeal approach. That's because many different institutions have an impact on caregivers today. These changes — singly or together — won't provide a comprehensive solution to the problems caregivers face. But any one of them will be an enormous step forward. And all of them can be achieved, now, within already existing institutional frameworks.

Reform #1: Make Respite Care Widely Available and Affordable Through State and Federal Legislation

We use the term "respite care" here in its broadest sense — sufficient relief from the 24-hour-a-day, 7-day week of caregiving. It might mean a 24-hour attendant to give the caregiver a day, weekend, or week off. It might mean an aide who comes in four hours per day to bathe and groom the disabled older person and prepare a meal. It might mean the patient going to an adult day care center one day per week or five, or to a nursing home or residential care home for several days or as much as a month. It might also mean as little as a sitter coming in for a few hours every other week. Respite services need to be provided in a manner that meets each caregiver's needs, and that is consonant with and respectful toward her cultural background.

Currently, respite services are available in a wide variety of ways. Profit-making firms offer some at high cost. Churches and social service agencies provide respite in the home (often done by volunteers). Government funding provides respite in some cases: through Medicare and Medicaid—in limited cases, like demonstration (model) programs in some states—or the Medicare hospice benefit; through local and statewide model programs on a sliding scale basis (eligibility requirements vary); through In-Home Supportive Services programs (although in some states, only elders with no family caregiver can get these services); through the Veterans Administration in some locations.

Respite care is often too expensive, is not sufficient to meet the caregiver's needs, is available only to a narrowly defined group, or all three. The complicated service picture constantly changes. Demonstration programs start up, funded by the government or foundations. They give services for a few years, then leave the caregivers with nothing when the demonstration period ends. Medicare and Medicaid regulations are often revised. Good local projects start up and are sacrificed to local funding cuts.

The solution is permanent change in the laws governing health care programs, not just temporary programs, and services that are universally available, not just for the lucky few.

Action on the state level could go a long way toward making respite care more available and affordable. The Older Women's League has developed a model bill on respite, which has been introduced into a number of state legislatures and passed in adapted form in several states. Under the bill, respite care would be made available on a sliding fee scale. There would be a number of options: the respite could be in the home, in an adult day health center, or an overnight or weekend in a nursing home. The fees would range from no cost if the patient were on SSI, gradually sliding up to the full fee for a patient with an income of 200 percent of SSI.

It is important that the *patient's* income be the basis for the sliding scale fee; if the basis is the income of an adult child caregiver who shares a home with the patient, that will mean adult children will often pay more for respite in the home than they would if their parent were in a nursing home (where Medicaid will step in if the parent's income is low, and the adult child's income does not count). Any financing plan that makes nursing home care cheaper than respite care just reinforces society's present bias in favor of nursing home care.

In some areas of New York State, respite is provided under a comprehensive plan called Nursing Home Without Walls. The program provides a wide range of services, including medical care and personal care, to people who would otherwise have to live in nursing homes. The services are provided on a sliding fee basis and Medicaid patients can receive services if the cost is less than 75 percent of the cost of a nursing home. The Nursing Home Without Walls model has the advantage of providing respite as part of a comprehensive program of care that is aimed at meeting the needs of the disabled person, the caregiver, and the rest of the family.

On the federal level, an important reform would be covering respite services under Medicare and Medicaid. Who would decide how much respite a caregiver should have? One possibility would be for the physician caring for the disabled elder to make the determination. A method that might make more sense would be for the "gatekeeper" to be a case manager, such as a social worker or nurse. (See Chapter 7 for a description of case management.) A case manager could certify that the caregiver needs the services and also keep track of where the services could be obtained, advising the caregiver as to how to arrange for them. This is a better plan than specifying a certain number of respite hours per month, because the needs of each disabled older person and each caregiver are different. If the goal is to allow people who want to be caregivers to provide the best care they can at home (rather than in a nursing home), respite services should be reimbursed under Medicare/Medicaid adequately, so that they will allow the caregiver to meet that goal.

Making respite services reimbursable under Medicare and Medicaid will stimulate providers of respite care service, either private enterprise or government-funded, if the rates are adequate (as they should be). Additional government funding may be needed to provide start-up funds for nonprofit programs like adult day care centers.

On the level of the private sector, respite services should be added to the health care services already covered (and reimbursed) under private health insurance.

Reform #2: Prevent the Impoverishment of the Caregiving Spouse

When a husband gets Alzheimer's disease or another chronic degenerative disease, it's a catastrophe for the couple. It should not be compounded by the couple having to "spend down" all their assets in order to qualify the husband for Medicaid nursing home benefits. The specter of impoverishment keeps many a middle-income woman providing care at home long past the time when she is physically capable of doing it.

As we saw in Chapter 3, the kind of care needed by people with chronic diseases—called long-term care or "custodial care" — is not covered by Medicare or private insurance (with a few exceptions). Once nursing home care becomes necessary, the cost is between $1,800 and $3,000 per month. At that rate, it takes less than three years to wipe out a couple's savings of $50,000 when the husband enters a nursing home. Only when their savings are down to $3,400 do they get Medicaid coverage for a portion of the nursing home care. A wife may care for her husband as long as she can, perhaps harming her own health in the process. Finally, she places her husband in a nursing home, with no financial help until she reaches poverty. She may then live on another 20 years — with no opportunity to rise out of poverty.

California law currently provides for an automatic separation of assets when one member of the couple enters a nursing home. This means that when one-half of the couple's marital or community property assets have been "spent down," Medicaid coverage for nursing home care begins. A few other states allow couples to sign a separation of assets agreement. At least half of a couple's assets should be protected from Medicaid "spend-down" requirements in every state.

At least half of the couple's monthly income should also be protected. A pension in the husband's name should be divided equally between husband and wife when the husband enters a nursing home. As it stands now, to qualify for Medicaid assistance in paying for nursing home care, the couple must spend almost all their monthly income on it. The wife is only allowed a small "maintenance allowance," far below the poverty line.

A separation of assets and income should be an option at the onset of disability. Otherwise, there will be a bias toward nursing home care. A patient might well be ineligible for Medicaid-financed services in the home or community (because the couple's assets and income were too high). He would, however, become eligible for Medicaid-financed nursing home care, because once he entered a nursing home there would be a division of assets and income.

The Older Women's League has prepared model state legislation to prevent the impoverishment of the caregiving spouse for introduction in states that do not as yet allow separation of assets in determining Medicaid eligibility for a spouse in a nursing home. The Older Women's League is also working for changes in federal law, so that states that enact laws to help caregiving spouses will not be penalized by the loss of federal Medicaid funds.

Reform #3: Cover Long-term Care for Chronic Illness—in Nursing Homes, in the Community, and in the Home—under Medicare

When Medicare was established in 1965, the issue of including long-term care was discussed by Congress. It was dropped because of the potential cost to government. But with roughly 70 percent of all people in nursing homes on Medicaid, the government is *already* paying almost half of the cost of long-term care. But because Medicaid is a welfare program, government aid comes only at great psychological and financial cost, due to the need to become poor in order to qualify.

Today, we are in an era of potential and actual Medicare cutbacks. Medicare regulations are, in fact, putting a greater burden on caregivers. People are being sent home from the hospital "sicker and quicker," often too sick to qualify for Medicare home care. Under these conditions a broad expansion of Medicare benefits may not seem politically feasible.

But there may be ways to fund long-term care under Medicare without bankrupting the fund. Increased general revenue funding or higher Social Security payroll taxes could cover a portion of the cost. These are some other possibilities:

1. Allow all Medicare beneficiaries to pay higher premiums, perhaps on a sliding scale basis based on income, in order to get long-term care coverage. For example, a 10 percent income tax surcharge would affect high income elders more than those with low income. This proposal is not universally acceptable among aging advocates.

2. Reinstate a federal estate tax for persons dying after age 65 when there is no living husband or wife. This would affect wealthier elders more than others.

3. Create an optional policy the Medicare recipient could purchase, available free to those on Medicaid.

Although many people on Medicare would not want to pay more, polls have shown that most would be willing to pay something for the assurance that they (and their spouses) would not face poverty if they had a long-term chronic illness.

Reform #4: Overhaul SSI and Medicaid

As we have described, American public policy forces middle-income caregivers to keep providing care as long as possible to avoid impoverishment. Paradoxically, public policy also discourages family caregiving among the poor; it provides strong incentives for putting poor elders in nursing homes while giving little or no support for care at home. In fact, in some cases, caregivers are actually penalized financially for caring for their relatives at home.

Welfare programs should be overhauled so that low-income people who want to care for their relatives at home are encouraged to do so.

First, the Supplemental Security Income program (SSI) should have its disincentive for family caregiving removed. SSI is a federal program that provides monthly income to people over 65 (and also to blind and disabled people of any age) who have very low or no income and very limited assets. Some states supplement the basic monthly benefit. Depending on the state, the maximum monthly amount in 1986 ranged from $336 to $553 for an individual, $504 to $989 for a couple.

The problem for a caregiving daughter (or son) is that the parent's SSI payment is *reduced by one-third* if he or she moves into the adult child's home to be cared for. But the *full cost* of the elderly parent's nursing home care would be covered by Medicaid.

The adult children of low income elders frequently have low incomes themselves. The full SSI payment may be an important part of the family income if the younger generation wants to provide care at home. A disabled adult who is on SSI should not have the benefit reduced simply because he or she moves in with an adult child who provides care.

Second, Medicaid needs to be reformed to reverse its bias toward nursing home care. Medicaid is a joint federal-state program that pays for health care for poor elders and certain other people who qualify. Elders on SSI are automatically covered by Medicaid; they are "categorically needy." Many other older people qualify for Medicaid. If their income is too high for SSI benefits, but they have high medical bills, they can become eligible as "medically needy." The most common way for this to happen is after "spending down" for nursing home care, as described earlier.

Medicaid's bias toward nursing home care operates in several ways. In many states, the only way for a disabled elder to be eligible for "medically needy" benefits is to enter a nursing home. A person receiving care at home receives no help with medical bills, no matter how high (although Medicare may provide some help, in some cases). The law should guarantee that Medicaid will pay medical bills for "medically needy" people being cared for at home, as it does for those in nursing homes.

In addition, in most states, Medicaid recipients are covered for acute hospital care or care in a nursing home, but for little or no care that would help them if they are being cared for by a family member. Services such as home medical care or respite for the caregiver are seldom covered. This means a caregiver faces an uphill battle if she wants to care for a Medicaid-eligible relative at home. The law should guarantee that nursing care and social services at home—including such services as case management, respite and home-delivered meals—are available to Medicaid recipients in every state. Home care costs should be reimbursed as long as they are lower than the cost of caring for that patient in a nursing home.

Reversing Medicaid's bias toward nursing home care is one reform that will probably lower the cost to government, since under present regulations, poor people have a strong incentive to choose the most expensive type of care for their older relatives —care in a nursing home.

Another problem with Medicaid is that it penalizes "medically needy" older people by forcing them to pay a monthly "share of cost" before they are eligible for Medicaid funding for medical bills or nursing home costs. They pay all their income above a basic amount that the state deems necessary for living expenses. Usually, what is left the spouse who is not in a nursing home is so small that she can barely survive. Often, the amount left to her is less than the income level of a single person receiving SSI. The injustice is clear: in order to qualify for Medicaid funding, a person with an income is forced to live on less than a person on welfare.

Further, in some states, "medically needy" people are eligible for less health care coverage than "categorically needy" people. "Medically needy" Medicaid recipients should be given the same services as "categorically needy" recipients and be allowed to keep enough of their income so they are at least as well off as SSI recipients.

A final problem with Medicaid is that, with few exceptions, physicians, hospitals, pharmacists, and nursing homes are not *required* to provide care for Medicaid recipients. Discrimination by nursing homes against Medicaid recipients is rampant. A husband may enter a nursing home, spend down all the couple's assets, and qualify for Medicaid. The nursing home, even if it is a Medicaid provider, may then unlawfully refuse to keep him. All too often, the only nursing home that will accept him on Medicaid is fifty miles away, offers poorer care, or both. A nursing home that participates in the Medicaid program and that accepts a private paying patient should be *required* to keep caring for that patient when he or she becomes eligible for Medicaid. State agencies should enforce the federal law prohibiting transfer of patients converting to Medicaid. Moreover, nursing homes should be required to accept Medicaid patients on a non-discriminatory basis. The Older Women's League has prepared a model state bill on preventing nursing home discrimination against Medicaid patients.

Reform #5: Provide Tax Incentives for Caregivers

Currently, *employed* taxpayers are eligible for credit on their federal income tax for expenses incurred caring for a disabled adult at home. The tax credit in 1986 was a maximum of $720, based on a sliding income scale. Bills have been introduced in Congress to give this tax credit to nonworking caregivers, but they have not passed.

Extending a tax credit to nonworking taxpayers would be a good step. It would benefit some, but not all, caregivers. Tax credits (which are amounts subtracted from taxes owed) tend to benefit the middle class most. Tax deductions (which are amounts deducted from taxable income) are of most benefit to the wealthy. Low-income caregivers with little or no tax liability are not helped by tax incentives, but they could be helped by a refundable tax credit, which would be an even better step.

In the modest amounts proposed ($500 - $1,000), tax credits will not change the mind of a caregiver who does not want to provide care at home. Though the tax credit can be used to finance some paid caregiving services, the amount is too small to make up for the loss of income to a woman who gives up paid employment for full-time caregiving. However, for middle-income caregivers whose financial situation is made more difficult because of the cost of caregiving, the tax credit could be a real help.

Tax incentives could also be useful in the area of housing. Many families would like to care for a disabled parent at home, but would have to add a room to their house to do so. It may also be necessary to modify a house by adding features such as

162

wheelchair ramps. A tax credit, or a subsidized construction loan, would help some caregivers who want to provide care at home avoid having to put their relative into a nursing home.

Reform #6: Increase the Availability of Comprehensive Private Health Insurance for Long-term Care

This type of coverage was unavailable a few years ago, but now insurers are cautiously getting into the field. However, the direction most of them seem to be taking is to cover only nursing home care. This is because they want, in their terms, a "well-defined trigger event," for starting to pay benefits. Entering a nursing home is such a trigger event; they consider the need for care at home or in the community a poorly defined trigger event. They also prefer to have a trigger event that people want to avoid; since most caregivers postpone turning to a nursing home as long as possible, this delays the date when benefits will have to be paid. However, it would be a tragedy if this trend continues. Long-term health care insurance will then become one more factor that gives the caregiver only the stark choice of coping all by herself, with no financial help for services, or putting her relative in a nursing home where some or all of the cost will be covered.

A "Reform" That Will Just Make the Problem Worse: "Relative Responsibility"

During the 1980s, some politicians have put forward the idea that families should do more to care for disabled older relatives. In particular, they are concerned about the escalating Medicaid nursing home bill, and they want families to be required to pay for nursing home care if an older individual is no longer able to do so. Some states, such as Idaho, have passed laws to try to make relatives financially responsible for nursing home payment.

163

So far, the courts have not upheld these laws, but states continue to try to come up with an acceptable proposal.

The idea of relatives being legally responsible to provide or pay for care raises many questions. Who in the family should be responsible? Are we talking again about the relative who was a principal caregiver for several years, prior to the institutionalization of the disabled person? Or are we talking about an extended family? Children, brothers and sisters, cousins, nieces and nephews? Where would we stop? Step-children? Children of a divorce, whom the institutionalized person hasn't seen in years? Children who were abused by this parent? And what about the children who live in another state?

So far, states that want to enforce "relative responsibility" laws haven't come up with a way to reach children living in another state. The consequence is that children who want a frail parent to move into their state so they can help provide care for her or him may be reluctant to arrange the move, for fear that when the parent enters a nursing home, they will be held liable for the costs. Or, a more extreme case, children might flee the state in order to avoid this financial obligation. What a strain on family relationships!

There is a further practical problem: if there are several children, how would the financial burden be assessed? Equally among them, or according to the income of the children? What if some of the children have children of their own whom they are supporting and others have no children? Either way, we have another strain on sibling relationships.

In many cases, poor parents have children whose income is likewise low. The burden of relative responsibility laws will fall predominantly on lower income families. They will be supporting their own children at the time they are called on to support their parents in nursing homes. One possible consequence of such pressure is that they will be rendered unable to save for their own retirement, and the cycle of poverty in old age continues.

Administrative difficulties will be common with relative responsibility laws. Many studies indicate that the costs of going after families to obtain their share of the cost of care for their parents would be so great that there would be little saving for the state. And what if family members refuse to pay their share? Would the parent in the nursing home be punished by being denied Medicaid benefits?

The way to encourage families to provide care is not through "relative responsibility" laws. Families already want to provide a lot of help and care. What is necessary is a partnership between families and society—a partnership that will offer families community-based services with a sliding scale fee that will help them give the care they are already trying to provide.

Pointing the Way to More Comprehensive Solutions

As more and more older women become caregivers, we need to look at the future. Following are some models for providing a comprehensive, integrated system of long-term health care in a way that will enhance and assist family caregivers.

S/HMO

S/HMO is the rather cumbersome acronym for Social/Health Maintenance Organization. It is a concept that builds on the existing model of the Health Maintenance Organization (HMO). An HMO is a prepaid health plan. Instead of paying for each visit to a physician or hospital, the members pay a monthly or quarterly fee. Health care services covered by the plan are then provided at a nominal or no cost. HMOs have a strong incentive to keep their members healthy, since the HMO takes in the same fee, no matter how many health services the member needs. HMOs are becoming increasingly popular and more are springing up around the country. The oldest and best known is the Kaiser Permanente system on the West Coast. Most members do not pay their own monthly fees. The fees are usually paid as a benefit of employment, by the employer, in place of a traditional health insurance policy. Members over 65 can have part of the fee covered by Medicare. They may pay the additional cost themselves; sometimes all or part is paid by an employer, even after retirement.

HMOs generally offer only the kind of medical services that are covered by Medicare. They seldom cover long term chronic care of the type provided by family caregivers although some do provide hospice care. The S/HMO takes the HMO concept a step further, providing long-term chronic health care to members.

S/HMO services, in theory, would be available to members whether or not they had family caregivers. An S/HMO could provide all the services necessary to keep a chronically ill older person comfortable at home (or in an institution that was affiliated with the S/HMO). Respite services for family caregivers could be included. Providing these services would, in most cases, be more cost-effective for the S/HMO than providing all the care the patient needed.

S/HMOs could be financed in ways similar to the present financing of HMOs. Monthly or quarterly fees could be a benefit of employment. If the long-term services were reimbursable under Medicare (as they should be), S/HMO could be one option for anyone eligible for Medicare, with the additional cost of the premiums financed as it is at present, by an individual or a past employer.

The federal government is presently experimenting with several S/HMOs for Medicaid recipients in various cities around the country. These S/HMOs provide both acute medical care and what the regulations refer to as "custodial" care. They also provide services such as case management, transportation, home-delivered meals, and respite care.

As with other current federally-funded demonstration programs, the government is concerned that the total cost for all members not exceed what the cost would be if the program did not exist. The point of demonstrations is to determine if long-term care services provided through a S/HMO can be less expensive than keeping Medicaid recipients in nursing homes. Thus, there is a danger that the S/HMOs will try to enroll primarily healthier older people, who need less care. Nevertheless, these projects are an important model for the future, providing a wide range of services not otherwise available. They help keep older people who would otherwise have to go to nursing homes living in their communities. S/HMOs could provide both maximum care for the disabled older person and adequate help for the caregiver. If the S/HMO is found to be a cost-effective alternative to the nursing home for people on Medicaid, it will point the way to wider availability of this model for other older people, too.

Expanded Hospice Services

Hospice care is one of the newest human services in this country. While services may vary, the essential focus of every hospice program is to give terminally ill patients the option of remaining free from pain and in a home environment as long as possible. The emphasis is on care, not cure. In the approximately 1,500 hospice programs currently operating today, a basic set of care elements is usually made available 24 hours a day, 7 days a week. These include:

1. Care rendered by a professional interdisciplinary team that works with an attending physician.

2. Use of volunteers as an integral part of that team approach.

3. A coordinated, comprehensive plan for home care and in-patient care.

4. Attention to support needs of both the patient and the family, with emphasis on practical, emotional, and spiritual needs.

Hospice, unlike traditional medical care, is a system that makes the patient as comfortable and content as possible. Pain medication is administered without the fear of addiction, and hospice nurses usually are experienced in dealing with the side effects of pain killers—lack of appetite, constipation, and nausea. They can help train family members to deal with these problems so that the feeling of caring is shared without the caregiver being burdened or feeling helpless. The subject of death is not avoided. From a dying patient's point of view, hospices provide support for whatever that person needs to do to make death less traumatic. From the family's point of view, adjustment to life without the patient begins long before death and often requires professional treatment and guidance. And another characteristic of a good hospice plan is offering bereavement follow-up to the family after the death of the patient.

Generally speaking, a hospice team includes a combination of professionals — nurses, social workers, home health aides, physical therapist, cancer specialist — and trained volunteers. The volunteers are specially selected and augment staff services and are not there in lieu of staff. They provide vital non-medical services—companionship, transportation, and respite periods for the family caregivers. Once a week, the entire team gathers to go over the patient reports with the directing physician. If there are special patient problems, the team considers possible solutions for the charge nurse to employ.

An expanded hospice program could be a good model for care for the chronically ill. As things stand now, however, there are restrictions on hospice care, especially under the Medicare hospice benefit. Often, hospice is available only to people who have terminal cancer and less than six months to live.

The key concept that makes hospice a useful model for an expanded long-term health care system is "palliative care." Medicare regulations dismiss with the term "custodial" all medical services that make a patient with a long-term illness as healthy and comfortable as possible. If it doesn't cure or improve an acute illness, it's not ordinarily covered, according to Medicare. (Medicare does cover hospice services for terminally ill cancer patients, and will do so as long as it proves cost-effective.) Hospice begins from the premise that the patient will not recover, and that what is needed is palliative care. Palliative care makes the person feel better, makes the disease more bearable, alleviates pain and prevents complications. Palliative care may include services from a physician or nurse, but it also covers all the services caregivers normally provide.

Several aspects of the hospice model, if they were more widely applied, could help caregivers whose disabled relatives suffer from illnesses other than cancer, and for periods longer than six months. The creative use of volunteers makes hospice a cost-effective model on which to base a long-term health care system. The access to many services through one hospice worker also makes it an effective model for the caregiver. The central values of compassion, preserving the patient's dignity, and attention to the caregiver's emotional/physical needs could lead to a more humane chronic health care system more than any other model.

There's no reason why hospice should be limited to patients with a clear prognosis of less than six months to live. Experimenting with a wider scale hospice model could well be the key to a workable long-term health care system for the nation. Currently, however, even the 1,500 hospice programs don't begin to meet the needs of cancer patients being released from hospitals under new Medicare regulations "quicker and sicker." Adequate reimbursement from both the public and private sectors is essential to the growth of new programs. Unless or until that happens, only individuals who can afford hospice care or who can meet the Medicare eligibility requirements will get it, and the promising model of hospice for long-term chronic illness will remain confined to the smaller sector of terminal patients.

National Health Care System

In the long run, the only protection from the catastrophe of long-term chronic illness is a system of national health care. Medicare was enacted on the premise that elderly Americans should not have to go without health care because they can't afford it. But what about people under 65? Under the present patchwork system, some people under 65 have health care coverage through employment, some through welfare, some buy their own, and some have none at all. Employment-based coverage can end if chronic illness causes loss of the job; the only choice may be paying very high premiums for continued coverage at a time when income has been drastically reduced by the illness.

Disabling illnesses do not respect the magic age of 65; they can strike at younger ages. And even if they do come after age 65, as we have seen in Chapter 3, most of the cost of caring for a person with a chronic illness is not covered by Medicare anyway. Nor is it covered, for a person of any age, by most health insurance plans.

America is the only industrialized country in the world that doesn't have a national health plan (either national health insurance, as in Canada, or a national health service, as in Britain). A comprehensive solution to the problems of the caregiver lies in a national health plan—one that covers palliative care for chronic illnesses, as well as acute care.

Winning Reforms: the Time Is Right for a Caregiver's Movement

Today's caregivers know what changes they need most, and they are also the ones who can make the best case for them. If every caregiver were to tell her story to a church group, in a letter to the editor, at a civic group, to a woman's organization, to a class of medical students, and not least, to her state and federal legislators, there would be a sudden and dramatic change of policy on aging. The caregiver question would dominate the

170

media and politicians would jump on the bandwagon. Funds would be found from both public and private sources to initiate respite care and other services. Medicare and Medicaid rules would be changed so that caregivers need not become impoverished. Some of the best minds would address the problem of care for the chronically ill. But caregivers have been facing their problems in isolation. Some social workers and gerontologists have talked about the problems, but they are not always taken seriously by policy makers. Caregivers themselves are the most effective spokespersons.

When Clemmie Barry founded Women Who Care, a pioneering support group for wives caring for disabled husbands, in 1977, she wrote: "First, I would hope that there might be immediate help, just in the sharing. Then I would hope that we could collectively find our voice and make it heard. As we define our needs specifically with our shared thinking, I am sure that change will come."

This was indeed the pattern of the group that followed. First, the sharing, then the collective voice, and finally the steps that brought significant relief. Relief came in the form of three years of foundation funding for the Wives' Respite Project. The members of Women Who Care went after, and got, the funds they needed for three things they saw the need for:

1. *Home Care*. A full-time nurse divided her time each week among the 10 - 15 wives in the group who asked for her service. There was no charge to the wives. The nurse provided care at home, giving the wives a break, and also performed services like bathing the disabled husband and monitoring his medical condition.

2. *Overnight Respite*. A 6-bed facility was set up at a renovated seminary conference center and staffed by professionals over a long weekend to give the group members up to four days of respite.

3. *Community Education*. Women Who Care worked with a

local community videotape group to produce a video, "Women Who Care: Living With Disabled Husbands." It has been shown to many community groups, aired on cable television, and shown to grantmakers. The video has also led to the group getting national media attention.

But the steps from sharing to finding a collective voice to making changes do not happen automatically. The emotional strains and time pressures are so great that just making it to a support group to share experiences can be a formidable hurdle. Then, to decide to speak about such a personal problem in a public way—like appearing on a television program or testifying before a legislative committee—is another giant step. To become involved in advocacy long enough to help get a respite program or an adult day care center may seem almost impossible.

Yet there are good reasons why it is worthwhile to travel along these three steps. A shared burden is rarely as heavy as one carried alone. To feel a victim of circumstances and to do nothing to improve those circumstances only leads to helplessness, hopelessness, and depression. When groups of women like those in Women Who Care really understand the scope of the problem and its social ramifications, the personal guilt dissipates. When they take the next step of action to alleviate the problems they share with others, they are transformed from victims of circumstance to healers of social wrongs. Their self-image improves, their moods lighten, and new energy is generated. Sharing a problem, raising the consciousness of others, and designing solutions to help not only themselves but many others is good for all concerned—the caregivers, the people they care for, and society as a whole. For with solutions in place, others need not experience the same isolation and despair. As one woman said at her mother's funeral, "Let my suffering not be in vain. If out of it emerges a better way of handling our aging and feeble parents, it will have been worth it."

Caregivers will need help in this process. And they have a

tremendous potential resource for help and empowerment in agencies that serve them. Agencies like adult day care centers and senior centers can become the nucleus and focal point for organizing advocacy. The members of Women Who Care have the support and assistance of Marin Senior Day Services, and the interaction of the two has added up to more than the sum of the parts.

Every community is ripe with opportunities for raising consciousness about the problems caregivers face. Wherever possible, caregivers should be spokespersons, telling their stories first hand. Agency staff can best serve as facilitators . . . identifying opportunities for caregivers to make their concerns known . . . providing transportation and respite care so the caregiver can take part in a community meeting or legislative hearing . . . making arrangements, for example, for a caregiver to get a convenient time slot on a hearing agenda. These hearings may start early in the morning and go on into the late hours of the night. It is almost impossible for caregivers to be away from home at these hours, nor can they wait hours to give fifteen minutes of testimony. Agency staff can also be helpful in dealing with funding sources. Marin Senior Day Services staff had the expertise in grantwriting that allowed Women Who Care to get funding for the Wives' Respite Project.

There are a number of government bodies in which caregivers can be an influence. Caregiver groups can arrange a meeting with state legislators, congressional representatives, the mayor, members of the city council or county board of supervisors, or directors of county departments of social service, aging, health, or mental health. There are also government and government-regulated bodies that have regular meetings where caregivers can get on the agenda: local health planning councils, long-term care planning committees, Area Agencies on Aging and their advisory boards (often called the Commission on Aging or Council on Aging), and local Commissions on the Status of

Women. These commissions and planning councils may also hold hearings for public input on specific topics, plans or funding proposals. Caregiver advocacy may influence the allocation of resources.

Occasionally, there are opportunities for caregivers and their agency allies to advocate on a regional, state, or national level. For example, caregivers have testified in the California State Legislature at hearings on bills on adult day care and respite care.

Caregivers can also tell their stories at meetings of voluntary organizations that may go on to join them in advocating for change. These include local chapters of the Older Women's League, National Women's Political Caucus, National Organization for Women, Gray Panthers, American Association of Retired Persons, National Council of Senior Citizens, and service organizations such as Zonta, Soroptimists, and American Association of University Women.

Media is, of course, another powerful way to get the caregiver's message across. Members of Women Who Care have done public service announcements on local television and radio about the need for respite care. Articles in local papers are useful. The best way to get them is not to wait for the papers to call, but to establish contact with a journalist and try to interest him or her in the human interest angle of a caregiver's story. Send press releases about support group meetings and special events. Caregivers can also contact hosts/hostesses or producers of local TV and radio talk shows and arrange to appear on them.

A caregiver support group can also sponsor its own workshop for health care practitioners and the general community. Invite physicians, discharge planners, social workers and grantmakers to be on the panel. This is a good way to get key people to participate, and they can then be educated about the problems and action needed.

The time is right for a caregivers' movement. There have been enough effective programs on television and enough organizing of support groups to lay the groundwork for a major break-through of consciousness. At least one organization, the Alzheimer's Disease and Related Disorders Association (ADRDA) has mobilized families nationally with chapters across the country. Its effective advocacy has brought about unprecedented attention to what has been called "the silent epidemic" and the momentum is continuing to build. Alzheimer's disease has moved from the confines of medical journals to national attention. Advocacy has led to major TV dramas and documentaries on the issue being shown nationwide, increased funding for research, and other benefits.

The ADRDA model of advocacy is focused on the disease itself. This has been necessary because, until the public became familiar with the illness and its consequences, there could be no substantial progress, either for a cure and adequate care, or for alleviation of the suffering of family members. Other organizations focus on stroke, cancer, Parkinson's disease and many other illnesses.

While these organizations can be of some help to caregivers, they inevitably stress the illness and those who suffer from it, sometimes neglecting the impact of that illness on the caregiver and the rest of the family. When one person becomes chronically ill, there are many consequences and most of them are not medical in nature. Personal relationships are disrupted, work patterns change, money must be expended differently and households are torn apart. These impacts are little noted except by those who experience them, and so they remain invisible except to those most directly affected.

We need advocacy that will put the needs of the caregiver first, in order to bring to light the social consequences of the chronic illnesses that plague an aging population. The point of this advocacy is to make the problems of the caregiver open to public scrutiny. It is to make it clear to every woman that she may well walk in the same shoes as the woman who now cares for her husband or parent in her home, perhaps losing her health, social life and income in the process. It is to make the problem real and personal to policy makers, the media and the public, so that the spotlight on the caregiver can pave the way for beneficial reform.

9

A Proposal for a Partnership:

Making Caregiver Values Society's Values

Caring for someone you love through a final illness can be a deepening, rewarding experience. If the experience is freely chosen, if the caregiver gets support from medical professionals (training at her new tasks, answers to her questions, appropriate care for her relative from both doctors and nurses when necessary), if caregiving doesn't lead her into poverty, if she has help so that the work doesn't overwhelm her, if she gets some respite, if her family is supportive, if excellent care in an institution is available when she feels it is necessary and she is not made to feel guilty for choosing it, then caregiving can be a meaningful close to a loving relationship. It can be a rich, deep connection to the cycles of life and an experience that many people would not want to miss.

Today, however, most caregivers do not have any of these supports. They are left to cope in isolation, as best they can. And what could be a long and loving goodbye often becomes a desperate ordeal.

The basic question that faces us today is not, "Who will care for the growing numbers of chronically ill older people?" Many, many people (most of them women) really want to care for their parents, their spouse, their brother or sister. Rather, we are faced, as a society, with two basic questions. First, how can America make it possible for people to give care without carrying the tremendous burdens they now shoulder? Second, how do we make it morally possible for caregiving to be an option, freely chosen? The second question means that it must also be possible *not* to be a caregiver.

The Medical Model and the Value of Care

Modern medicine is so all-pervasive in our culture that we tend to forget just how recently it has come on the scene. Two hundred years ago, most health care was provided at home, by women. Caring for the sick was just one of the many skills that rural women had to possess; others were caring for children, gardening, preserving and preparing the family's food, spinning, weaving, and sewing the family's clothing, making candles and soap, and many more. Both men and women—for the most part and among most classes—worked on the land. Through their own skills, they directly produced most of their food, shelter, and other necessities, including medical care. The industrial revolution changed all that. America was transformed from a nation of households that produced most of what they consumed into a nation of households that bought almost everything with money earned on the job.

Modern medicine evolved as an expensive commodity—one of the most expensive that has to be purchased. Today the medical model of health care has the appearance of the natural order of things. But while much of what women formerly did has become a huge, high-tech industry driven by profit, some of the work of health care still remains for women to do in the home, unpaid. Care that is not high-tech, that does not cure, but is necessary for comfort and survival is what remains. And like so much work that society has left to women in the home, this care is undervalued. When it is done for pay, for instance, by a usually female aide in a nursing home, the work is rewarded with the minimum wage—or less.

Today, medical care has been priced out of the budget of many Americans. Health insurance as a benefit on the job was introduced after World War II to alleviate this budget crunch (and to counter calls for a national health plan). Medicare was introduced in the 60s to put medical care back within the reach of the elderly. Medicaid was developed to make it available to the poor. All these programs, because of the way they reimburse high-tech, institutional care at the expense of personal care and care in other settings, have created an inflationary behemoth that devours an ever-growing share of the health care dollar.

Medicare and most health insurance policies do not finance what is termed "custodial" care. The implication is that care not requiring the skills of a nurse or physician is not *really* health care. It is merely care required to keep the patient as comfortable as possible, with the least amount of deterioration in health, in minimal pain. A better term for this type of care is *palliative*, with its connotation of comfort, rather than warehousing. The biggest political struggle facing a movement to change the working conditions of caregivers is the struggle to make palliative care valued, no matter who is giving it or what level of skill is required.

Caregiving has attained its present low social value in the context of what Barbara Ehrenreich and Deirdre English call "the romantic solution." As women's productive work moved out of the home, the role of women changed. Women came to be seen as guardians of the home and the home as a refuge from the cold, uncaring, "bottom line" world of the marketplace. Women were charged with defending a little world at home where love and caring are paramount, in contrast to the corporate world,

179

which is increasingly dominated by money and self-interest. To defend that haven, women are supposed to provide nurturing and care for love, not for pay.

Something Has to Give

Today's realities are straining the "romantic solution." It was based on the model of a nuclear family, with a male bread-winner and a wife caring for children at home. If an older relative needed help, the home would be available. But today, most families do not fit this model. There are more single-parent families, career couples who don't have babies, midlife women living alone. More and more women have moved into the market economy themselves. Few women expect (and fewer find) that marriage guarantees a lifetime of economic security, which might enable them to provide caregiving on an unpaid basis. More and more women must earn their own keep (and increasingly, earn their children's keep) for most of their life-times. People are also having fewer children (which translates later into fewer daughters or daughters-in-law available to care for disabled parents) and are less likely to live near their parents.

While changes in the family mean that fewer women are leading lives that allow the "romantic solution" to the problem of caring for older relatives, there is a vast increase in the number of older people needing chronic care. Back when America was primarily rural, few people lived to an old age. Fewer still lived a long time with a chronic illness, and most of those who did needed care for fewer years than today. Modern medical science has done a miraculous job of keeping people alive to later ages. But it has done much less about caring for the growing popula-tion who can no longer care for themselves.

Women are increasingly responsible for earning a living at the same time as a growing number of older people need their unpaid care at home. Something has to give—and too often today, it is the individual caregiver herself.

Is it realistic to ask individual women to make up for what government, men, and the market economy do not provide?

Women are being assigned the social role of providing compassion and care, witout being given any of the resources to do it. Some women will not want to take on that role. And that must be their right, just as it is for men. But for the many who do, it is necessary to build a movement that can win the changes in social policy to give caregivers the resources to do the job.

This may sound like a call to heap more work on an already harassed and overworked group, to ask women to take the lead in social change when we already do almost all the work of unpaid care. But because we have been socialized to take on the task of creating a haven of compassion, today we are the experts. We can keep on doing it alone, without support. Or we can demand that society place compassion at the center of its values, and take the lead in bringing that about.

Bringing Compassion to the Center

Compassion must take the center stage in social policy because the only real solutions to the problems of the caregiver are social. As long as care for the chronically ill older people falls on "the family" (meaning women), unsupported by the rest of society, everyone is at the mercy of luck. Each of us may need care at the end of life. If we're lucky, someone will be ready and willing to do it, with love. If not, then what? And each of us may have the responsibility of caring for a spouse, sibling, or parent—perhaps more than once. If we're lucky, we'll manage without ruining our own health or finances, and our relative's disease won't be one of the nightmare ones, like Alzheimer's. But if not, then what?

Most Americans, when asked, believe that other people consign their older relatives to nursing homes, but that they themselves will do the right thing when the time comes and take care of "my mother and father." But people have widely varying resources for doing so, and older people need widely varying levels of care for vastly different periods of time. Until America can say we are willing to care for *all* of our mothers and fathers, we are playing roulette with most of our citizens' final years.

If we are serious about maintaining the family as a source of love, nurturing, compassion, and care, the family needs a support system. The support system should be based on two premises:

1. That it is only right that we give our older citizens the best care possible at the end of life; and
2. That providing this care is a shared responsibility between society and families.

The support system should include all of the services described in Chapter 7. It should include a greatly expanded program of training and 24-hour medical backup for caregivers, modeled on the hospice program. It must also include financial assistance to the family, where that is necessary.

Financial assistance until now has been limited to "incentives," such as tax credits, that supposedly encourage people to keep an older person at home who would otherwise enter a nursing home at public expense. But many families are already desperately doing everything they can to keep their relative out of a nursing home, and the current incentives are too small to change the minds of those who don't want to care for a relative at home. Financial assistance should instead be provided to make the care that is needed possible, without all the sacrifices caregivers now make.

It comes down to the question of whether we believe health care to the end of life is a right or a privilege. Consigning a huge area of health care (care for chronic illness) to the family makes it not a right, but a privilege for those who can afford it.

The Danger of Arguments Based on Cost-Effectiveness

Health care cannot be made a right, however, at no cost to government. In these times, it has become unfashionable to propose anything that involves new costs to government. Some advocates for an expanded system of long-term health care for the elderly (including more public financing of care at home) have argued for it on the basis of cost-effectiveness. More funding for care at home, according to this argument, translates into fewer people in nursing homes. Since nursing home care is usually the most expensive variety of long-term care, and since Medicaid (a public program) pays for 70 percent of nursing home patients, public money will be saved by funding more home care.

But this doesn't take into account what government analysts have termed the "woodwork effect." Providing more public money for care at home, they say, would encourage people who are now providing care for free to "come out of the woodwork," and get publicly-funded services. In the view of government analysts, these are people who don't really need services. But readers of this book will understand who is really in "the woodwork." *It is older women who are often sacrificing their livelihood, health, and economic future to provide care, alone and unaided.*

Arguments based on cost-effectiveness fail because providing *some help* is always more expensive than doing nothing. *And nothing is what most caregivers now receive.* The vast majority of chronically ill older people do not live in nursing homes. Rather, they are in the government analysts' "woodwork," cared for at home by unpaid, usually older women.

The assumption behind the woodwork argument is that people who have been able to manage without services do not need them. But before Social Security, people managed somehow. Perhaps they were hungry, or they died prematurely, but they managed. People who couldn't manage were sent to county poorhouses—places sufficiently terrible so that adult children would have a strong incentive to support their aging parents. Social Security was enacted to make old age less precarious, and to do it on a social level, not on the level of the family.

We need better services for caregivers for the same reasons. As long as we argue for home care based on cost-effectiveness, we will always be vulnerable to the woodwork argument. After all, the ultimate in cost-effectiveness is just to let people die. Or going one step further, a painless death pill could be issued to disabled older people who are without funds, family, or friends.

The moral surrender to the Reagan Administration's zeal for cutting social programs hasn't gone quite this far. But people who argue on the basis of cost-effectiveness are still answering the wrong question: "What is the cheapest way to keep a disabled older person alive?"

That is not the question this nation should be asking. Instead, the nation must begin, on a society-wide level, to ask the question the way millions of caregivers ask it everyday: "What is the best way we can all care for our nation's older disabled citizens?"

A New Partnership

In the *family*, this partnership means socializing boys and men to provide hands-on care for older relatives, just as girls and women are now socialized. It means that if older women must balance a career and caregiving, older men must start asking and answering the same painful questions in their own lives.

In the *private sector*, this partnership means developing programs such as long-term health care insurance (see Chapter 8), leaves of absence with no loss of pension credits for employees who take time off for caregiving (and making these leaves available to both male and female employees), part-time employment for people combining work with care, and funding for programs such as adult day care centers.

In the *voluntary and philanthropic sector*, this partnership means establishing model volunteer programs to assist caregivers. But there is a danger in well-intentioned efforts that substitute unpaid work by women volunteers for the unpaid work of women in the home, providing a little service instead of making changes in the health care system. Volunteers are an important part of a comprehensive system of support for caregivers, but they can't do it all, any more than voluntary programs have been able to solve the problems of the hungry and homeless in this country. Programs that utilize volunteers will be much more effective in the long run if they sensitize the volunteers to the need for a real program of long-term health care. The programs will do more good if volunteers give 50 percent of their time to advocacy and 50 percent to service, rather than just helping out in the home.

In the *public sector*, this partnership means a comprehensive program for long-term health care for the chronically ill, including a support program for caregivers providing economic assistance, when necessary, to make it all possible.

For *caregivers*, this partnership means building a movement with all available allies to make all these changes possible—to make compassion, not cost, our primary social value when it comes to our aging population.

Beginning to Win

How do we begin to fight for these changes, which seem utopian in the midst of the 1980s? Women can be a formidable force. We should not underestimate our power to move public opinion. If each caregiver begins by telling her own story, that will move public opinion a lot. And caregivers don't need to stand alone. We can find allies among professionals who work with the elderly and see these stories every day. We can find allies among the churches, especially in arguing that our country has a moral duty to its elderly that should not be overridden by concerns of cost. We should also call on organizations of older people and feminists, on foundations, on voluntary service organizations, and on corporations that take an interest in the issue.

Actually changing the situation of caregivers is not a matter of changing a few regulations. It involves confronting national priorities. Societies that spend less for the military spend more on caring for their older population. But what is the real meaning of national security? Is it a bigger arsenal, or the knowledge that each citizen will be entitled to the care he or she needs in old age? Can we afford to spend so lavishly on weapons if it means abandoning our disabled older citizens?

It would be naive to think we can win all these changes at once. But we can win small victories that will make the next step possible. Reforms, such as legislation to make respite care available and to prevent caregiving spouses from falling into poverty, are excellent places to start. Small steps have been won on this front already. We can also raise the caregiver issue in the public consciousness. When the public becomes aware of the dilemma of the caregiver, that will be the first step in shifting the public policy debate from arguments based on cost to arguments based on compassion.

For too long, caregivers have asked the compassionate question, and given the compassionate answer, all alone. Now it's time to insist that society face up to its share of the responsibility, to enter into a partnership with caregivers that will guarantee good care for all of us as we age.

10

A Final Word

The process of collaboratively writing *Women Take Care* was well underway when one of the principal authors, Tish Sommers, became so ill with cancer that she needed constant care. The other principal author, Laurie Shields, became her primary caregiver. For both women, the experience was a deepening of their understanding of the issue of caregiving. Tish's health was deteriorating rapidly when the two women began to write more personal accounts of their experience. Both knew that Tish had only a short time left. Tish taped her section and handed it to Laurie on October 12, 1985, saying, "There, that's the last thing I have to do." Six days later, she died.

... *from Laurie Shields*

I suppose most caregivers begin by being the "significant other" in someone's life, the person who accepts the inevitable responsibility early on to care for (or arrange care for) someone who can no longer help herself or himself. I have been a significant other and primary caregiver twice in my adult life. Both

times, it was a conscious choice, and both times love was the
motivating factor.

I married late. My husband was much older than I and had a
history of respiratory problems. He was a gentle, caring, loving
man. In the old-fashioned definition of the word "good," he was
a good husband and father. His daughter, Christine, was 3 years
old when her mother died and just 7 when we were married.
From the start, it was a close family. Because he was an actor,
there were opportunities for us to be together perhaps more
often than families where the traditional provider goes off to a
daily job.

But in time, the respiratory problems increased. There were
middle-of-the-night trips to the hospital by ambulance while I
held his hand and wished I could help him breathe more easily.
He hated the hospital stays and constantly argued to be released.
Each time the doctor dismissed him reluctantly, knowing the
only help at home would be me. Finally, after one very serious
seizure, the doctor refused to release him unless we promised to
have a nurse around the clock for at least three months. Fortunately, we had the money to do that. While it was a costly
learning experience, I am still grateful to those wonderful caring
women who took pains to teach me what I'd have to know to go
it alone: how to give injections, how to monitor his blood
pressure and pulse, how to recognize blockage of his bowels
and what to do about it. When to resort to powerful supposi-
tories to ease his breathing. How to bathe him in bed and how to
help him use the bedside commode with the least harm to my
back. And because of the heavy drug regimen he was on, how to
keep records of everything.

Those were professional skills. While I never matched the
ability of my "teachers," in time practice built up my confidence
and ability to cope with whatever happened. And as other
caregivers know, one develops ways to meet needs that may not
be found in the nursing books. For example, he had both good

and bad days during the last three years. On the good days, he chafed at being confined to the bedroom where two large tanks provided the constant flow of oxygen he required. (This was before the invention of portable tanks, which must be a godsend to both caregivers and patients with similar problems.) We needed to find a way to keep him hooked up to the stationary tanks and still be free to walk around through the house. I asked the oxygen suppliers if it would be possible to obtain rubber tubing in long lengths. Once we had that, it was as though he had a new lease on life. He could walk out and have breakfast with me. He watched the cat have her kittens in the butler's pantry. We could both sit in the library listening to music we loved, or visit with old friends.

But those happy forays declined as the disease progressed. In an effort to make the required bed rest more attractive, I suggested he begin to tell me all he could remember of his days in Ireland's National Theatre, the Abbey. I moved the furniture around and fixed a table and chair next to him so I could take notes. For a while, the distraction worked. His sense of recall was impressive, even though he frequently had a hard time remembering current detals of our lives. And he was a great storyteller! I found myself eager to start the sessions and covered many tablets with notes I promised I would use some day in a book.

But he also hit dark days when he would cry out in despair and wish for death. Those were especially difficult days for me, alone with him. I didn't want him to die. My head said it was going to happen; my heart kept saying, "Please, not yet."

There were few, if any, community services available for me to call on. But what was lacking was more than made up by family and friends. Our daughter, Christine, who by then was working as a volunteer in the Cesar Chavez farmworker program, would take time off and come home for visits in the early stages of his illness. Later, she simply moved back home to help. A dear friend with a love both for the theatre and for Arthur would come and spend hours talking with him about the Abbey. The woman who had cleaned house for us in Hollywood for years got on a bus in Los Angeles after she finished working on Friday and came to us 200 miles away in Santa Barbara, returning every Sunday after a week-end of getting the house back in order again. Another old friend, a professional masseuse, came periodically to give him a badly needed massage. My parents were frequent visitors and helped with my shopping, even though neither of them drove and it meant taking two buses to reach us.

Toward the end, Arthur's drugs were changed, and some were increased. This affected him mentally. In some ways this was the most difficult time for me. I learned to anticipate his needs and dealt with growing incontinence with almost total detachment. What I couldn't seem to handle was the absence of communication between us. I missed the intimacy of our shared exchanges and I wept for the person I'd lost who hadn't yet died. And then, as though he, too, knew something was wrong and needed to be changed, shortly before he died he refused to take any medication. Although weak and probably conscious of death being near, he was once again mentally competent. The afternoon before he died he took my hand, told me he loved me, and thanked me. With a trace of his old grin he added, "I don't think I could have taken care of you as well." Shortly after midnight, he died, ten days past my 50th birthday. I loved him very much.

Tish and I met first in 1975. I was looking for a job. She had a small project going, Jobs for Older Women. She was hoping to get legislation enacted that would provide employment training for middle-aged and older women, whom she called "displaced homemakers." There had been some signs of my having a social conscience as I was growing up, but except for a brief turn as a volunteer at Dorothy Day's House of Hospitality in New York, my awareness of the need for social change was limited to what I read. I read a lot about the civil rights movement. I approved the war on poverty. I talked a lot about what was wrong with racism. But what I wasn't doing until I met Tish was *acting* out my beliefs.

Tish opened my eyes to other "isms"— chiefly, ageism and its impact on women. It had never crossed my mind that growing older female was different from the way it was for men. Without her encouragement, I doubt I'd have found the courage of my convictions and learned to speak and act against the social inequities women encounter in both a male- and a youth-oriented society.

So the "free lance agitator," as she then described herself, recruited a "footloose organizer" and for eleven years we worked on the needs and concerns of middle-aged and older women. We found we worked well together, even though our individual styles were different. For nine of those years we also shared a home.

Working and sharing a home together strengthened the bonds of our friendship. Tish had had a bout with breast cancer twenty years earlier, but the possibility of recurrence seemed remote. Then, it did recur, in the late '70s. In 1983, when I found I also had breast cancer, that relationship deepened and we became "significant others" for one another. In the two years that followed, when it became obvious that her six-year fight as a stage 4 cancer patient might be drawing to a close, there was no question but what I would become her primary caregiver.

Tish had been, as was her wont, very up front about her cancer. I was certain she'd beat the odds, chiefly because she was so sure of herself. She taught me (and many doctors along the way) that one can and should question authority; she was always in charge of her medical situation. Nor was she shy about asking for or taking advice from both doctors and nurses, and she inspired respect and real caring for them. When it became necessary for her to have an ostomy appliance inserted, Lily

Salisbury, then part of the visiting nurses department of the hospital where Tish had been treated, began a series of visits to change and clean the catheter. She also recommended special ointments to relieve skin pain from urine, and methods for dealing with constipation caused by the spreading tumors. When the Medicare coverage of these monthly visits officially "ran out," Lily kept coming on her own time and was there whenever we needed her. And it was Lily who answered all of Tish's questions about the hospice program, which we would need when everyone agreed her condition was terminal.

This time, there were some things common to my earlier experience as a caregiver, and I was thankful that I'd had it. But the differences were more important. There was more help at hand for ordinary chores and, importantly, there was the hospice program.

Tish may well be the only patient accepted into a hospice home care program who announced to her doctor that she was ready for it, but first had to make a trip to New York and Washington, D.C. She would go to New York to talk to possible funders for the Older Women's League, and to meet with members of an advisory committee of the United Methodist Health and Human Services Division, to urge them to become advocates for older people. She would go to Washington to say her goodbyes to the Older Women's League Board members at what she guessed was the last executive committee meeting she would attend. I was with her when she calmly explained this to the doctor, and my admiration for him — already high — rose several points as he casually said, "Well, I would hope there aren't any more trips planned."

So, even before hospice personnel checked in with us, Tish's reputation as a maverick was well established. The hospice staff couldn't have been more helpful. A charge nurse, Rhonda Henson, came twice a week in the beginning. A volunteer, Susan Edinborough, was there whenever we needed her and sometimes showed up because she knew we'd need her! They produced equipment and gave me lessons on things that needed to be done if they weren't there. But the most reassuring part was knowing there was a nurse on duty 24 hours a day, including weekends. It became necessary to use a special catheter. They experimented until we got just the right one, and then taught me how to insert it. They epitomized what is best in the hospice program—treat the patient, yes, but help the patient and the family deal with death in a dignified way. For example, Rhonda usually took Friday off to go up to her cottage in the mountains. Knowing Tish was close to the end one Thursday, she said nothing, but told Susan to call her if she was needed. I called Susan when Tish died the next day, Friday, October 18. Both Susan and Rhonda were here within the hour. They were a support group for Tish and all who cared for her (and they still are for me).

There were differences in the patients, too. Arthur had passively accepted the end, although he fought hard to be able to die at home. Tish also wanted to die at home, but not before she finished a list of "to-do's," all of which involved the future of the Older Women's League. They included a last minute proposal for funding a project, a videotaped message to be played at the board of directors meeting she knew she wouldn't attend, a videotaped message to those attending OWL's national convention in 1986, and an outline of the memorial service she finally agreed could be held, along with a list of those she hoped would attend.

And there were her "goodbyes" to friends on a one-to-one basis. To each, she left a personal memento. She told them what it was and then gave them a job to do for OWL. There were instructions for me and what she hoped would happen in my future. She asked for (and got) my pledge to continue her work on bringing death and dying out of the shadows of fear, and to help broaden and expand hospice services across the country.

She deliberately withheld the pain control medicine her tortured body cried out for because she wanted to keep her mind clear "until the list is finished." But she was very human, too. One night after a very painful bout, she began to cry. I walked over to her bed, held her, and then she said, "I'm tired of being brave." Gently rocking her a bit, I softly whispered into her ear, "You don't have to be." Then I pulled back and grinned at her as I told her, "You can be my courageous coward." The contradiction in terms seemed to amuse her, and the tears stopped.

While all of the goodbyes were in process, I stubbornly held out. I wouldn't let her say it, and I wasn't about to, either. Perhaps the same reasoning made me refuse to have anything to do with the injections the pain control program demanded. I just knew I couldn't do it. I phoned an old friend in San Diego, Pat Huckle, who immediately made arrangements for others to cover her classes at the university and came up that same afternoon. Pat had never given injections, but she was a quick study. Rhonda, the hospice nurse, was very pleased with her "technique." Once the program began, Pat had to get up in the middle of the night to keep the injections on schedule.

The drugs took over. Friends took on shifts to relieve Pat and me, and I also slept in Tish's room at night. Although I guessed Tish knew someone was with her all the time, she was apparently comatose. By the second day, I couldn't stand it. I went over, called her by name, and said, "I guess it's time to say goodbye." I wasn't sure she heard me, but at least I wanted to say it. I was holding her when I felt her hands reach up to my face, by then covered with tears. I drew back and found her smiling, eyes open and clear as ever, for a moment. Then, with a final pat on my cheek as we kissed one another, she slipped back into what became a deep coma. Two mornings later, she simply stopped breathing.

Again, hospice members took over and did what I had no heart to do. They washed and prepared her body for the cremation she had ordered. They stripped the bed and threw out linens no longer usable. They went through and removed any drugs that might be lethal and they stacked supplies I might later want to give away. (Most of them I gave to the hospice program.) They escorted the funeral director and his helper up to the room. When Tish's body was brought down and out to the hearse, it was Rhonda and Susan who walked that last distance with her.

There were some other differences in my two caregiving experiences. I really was the primary caregiver for Arthur after our three months of professional help. In some ways my chosen role was made easier by the fact that I was younger and in good health. Granted, I would have welcomed the community services that were available for Tish, but even though caregiving for Arthur was for a longer period of time, I felt later that I had managed well.

In contrast, it's unfair to call myself Tish's primary caregiver. Many people loved, cared about, and cared for her, especially during the last three difficult months. In addition to the hospice services, friends volunteered and took over one and two hour periods of just sitting with her. People brought in prepared food that could be frozen and used as needed. Unexpectedly, the woman who owns the travel bureau we have long used showed up the Saturday before Tish died, when there was a houseful of people, with a baked leg of lamb and huge servings of salad, green beans, and rolls. The fact that the OWL office work continued on the first floor of our home meant there were people at hand during the week to run upstairs with a cup of tea or soup or just be there for any emergency. What a fitting tribute to her years of work for others it was, that seeing her through a death was a collective, feminist action.

Although I chose to be a caregiver twice, I can only echo Tish's strong stand on making caregiving an option women must feel free to reject without carrying a load of guilt. It's not a role that's everyone's cup of tea. We must work together to prevent society from force feeding it to women, simply because it is perceived to be a "woman's role."

...from Tish Sommers (October 12, 1985)

Laurie and I have been working on the issue of caregivers now for several years with the Older Women's League Task Force. In the process, we decided to move ahead and write this book. A collective book like this takes some time, and during that time, Laurie has become a caregiver and I have been the recipient of that care. I had had cancer before but it did not limit my activities. In the past months, it began to progress until finally I found myself needing a great deal of care. Laurie lovingly gave it to me. This could not help but deepen my concern on this issue. It has made me think of some aspects of the problem of caregivers in society that perhaps we did not stress enough in this book. I will try to make up for that now.

Laurie and I have been very fortunate to have the best caring situation. The part of the illness that required such intensive care lasted a short time, maybe three months. Before that, I could pretty much manage for myself. I had no loss of mentality. I was able to keep going to the end and interact with her, as well as with other people, in a loving way. But most important, we had a hospice for support. The hospice provided a nurse practitioner twice a week. She came in to give advice, to teach Laurie techniques, and to take care of the go-between with the medical profession, making sure that needed drugs were ordered. In addition, she made sure volunteers were available on call. Because we shared a home that was also used as work space for OWL, it was possible for me to continue working, even from bed. We had a great deal of loving support from many people who could not do enough for both of us.

I did learn some things from this experience. First of all,

196

support services are necessary. It was important to have that nurse practitioner who could be called at any time day or night, if necessary, between those two weekly visits. Weekends are a terrible time for caregivers if something goes wrong and they don't know what to do. They need somebody who can provide the assurance and the technical know-how and do what needs to be done in an emergency. The necessity for support services was the strongest lesson. The second was that there is a kernel of deep emotion brought about by this level of dependency, which opens up one human being to the other and the love deepens. If the affection is there already, it grows. It may develop when it wasn't there from the start.

I had to come to terms with two things. One was diminishing autonomy. I have always been a very autonomous person. I took care of myself in every way. I've been a leader; I've been a self-starter. I have worked with Laurie and with other people very closely but I was always very sure of my own autonomy. I had to give that up, down to the most basic details, step by step. The process of doing that, of handing that autonomy over to another person whom I trusted and loved, opened up for me another kind of experience. It was very enriching.

The other thing was coming to terms with death. I had known I had cancer for years but I wasn't facing the immediacy of it. I found that, in this stage, coming to terms with death could be joyful, as well as painful. It is another new area we, as women, can explore. I have felt myself, joyously, a role model for death. To face it, to work with it, plan for it, to share it and not to fear it. And I feel I have succeeded, and that has been very rewarding.

However, I stand firm on the danger of presuming that women will take on the caregiving role. Sacrifice can be noble, but men are missing something in this experience. The ability to nurture is not inborn, it's ingrained from childhood on. It's a product of social expectations, a mother's role, a woman's role, and particularly our responsibilities in the caring for our elders. I don't believe that sacrifice always deepens affection, especially when there's no option, when there's no help, or when that help is inadequate, or anytime when the burden is just too heavy to handle. Love doesn't grow when guilt is the motivator.

This problem of caregiving to the end of life belongs to our whole society. It belongs to women, to men, and certainly to the government. When love, not guilt, can be the basic motivation, then caregiving can be a positive experience. But that will only be possible if there is a real sharing of responsibility for caregiving, a program of real support, and if the choice not to be a caregiver is available. Winning this social partnership may seem like an impractical vision now with all the cuts in social services. But we can start now on one piece of it, and win it one step at a time. Keeping our vision in mind, we can accomplish that goal togther. We opened this book by saying the title, *Women Take Care*, is both a statement and a warning. Today, we women must take care that more and more of us are not thrust unprepared into a task that is too much for us.

Resources

by Ida VSW Red

Finding Services: Getting Started

Finding local services — such as home health care, adult day care, counseling, or a support group — may take some time and ingenuity. Some places to begin include:

Local Senior Centers: Many communities have these centers, which may be listed in the telephone book under "senior centers" or "senior citizens center," or they may be with city or county government listings. These centers may provide referrals to services, or they may know a good source of referrals.

Local Government Aging Offices: Many cities and counties have government offices that can point the way to services. These may be listed in the phone book under government office headings such as "Department of Aging," "Mayor's Office on Aging," "Mayor's Senior Citizen's Office," "Department of Social Services," "Social Services Division," "Senior Citizen's Division," or similar titles. Some offices can give very good information while others will know little about services in their area.

199

State Government Aging Offices: For rural areas, especially in sparsely populated states, a state government office may be able to give referrals for services. It will usually be located in the state capitol and listed under state government offices, such as "Department of Aging" or "Department of Social Services."

Local Hospitals: A social worker at a reputable hospital will often have good information about health-related services such as home health care and nursing homes.

Churches: Churches and social service agencies related to churches may provide both services and referrals.

Aids and Equipment

A Handbook for the Disabled: Ideas and Inventions for Easier Living, by Susan Lunt (New York: Scribner's, 1982) Devices and ideas to compensate for disabilities and allow active living; directory of equipment suppliers.

Self-Help Manual for Patients with Arthritis, published by the Arthritis Foundation, has many good ideas (see telephone directory for local office).

Why Didn't Somebody Tell Me About These Things? A Guide to Assistive Devices, by Lou Hamilton (Shawnee Mission, KS: Intercollegiate Press) describes aids for sufferers of amyotrophic lateral sclerosis.

ABLEDATA, National Rehabilitation Information Center (4407 8th Street NE, Washington, DC 20017, 202-635-5822) lists thousands of items, makes computer searches for specific devices and sources of supply.

ELECTRIC MOBILITY CORP. (591 Mantua Blvd., Seward, NJ 08080, 800-257-7955) specializes in electric ambulatory equipment.

ENRICHMENTS, INC. (P.O. Box 579, Hinsdale, IL 60521): free catalog of varied items.

FASHION ABLE (Box S, Rocky Hill, NJ 08553): free catalog of self-help items for independent living.

G. K. HALL & CO. (70 Lincoln Street, Boston, MA 02111-9985, 800-343-2806): free catalog of large-print books (also available at public libraries).

COMFORTABLY YOURS (52 West Hunter Avenue, Maywood, NJ 07607, 201-368-0400): free catalog of aids for easier living.

DR. LEONARD'S HEALTH CARE PRODUCTS (65 - 19th Street Brooklyn, NY 11232, 212-768-5943) sells many unusual, hard-to-find items.

HORTON & CONVERSE PHARMACY (2001 Santa Monica Blvd., Santa Monica, CA 90405, 213-829-1834) specializes in medical equipment and supplies.

MOBILMEDICAL (2001 Coldwater Canyon, North Hollywood, CA 91606, 213-506-4252) rents and sells hospital furnishings and equipment described in free brochure (many also offered by similar local suppliers that advertise in yellow pages of the telephone directory).

SEARS, ROEBUCK & CO. (check local telephone directory) issues free catalog of many home health care items for sale.

National Associations

Some of these national associations may have local chapters listed in your telephone directory.

General

AMERICAN ASSOCIATION OF RETIRED PERSONS (AARP)
(1909 K Street NW, Washington, DC 20049, 202-728-4300). Offers discounted health insurance, car rental, and hotel rates; sponsors community service programs and pre-retirement planning programs. 3,500 local groups; 10 regional groups. Publications: News Bulletin (monthly); Modern Maturity (bi-monthly); The Right Place at The Right Time; A Handbook About Care in the Home.

ASOCIACION NACIONAL PRO PERSONAS MAYORES (ANPPM)
also known as National Association for Hispanic Elderly (2727 W. Sixth Street Suite 270, Los Angeles, CA 90057, 213-487-1922). Articulates needs of Hispanic and other low-income elderly. Administers project to employ low-income people over age 55. 7 regional groups. Publications: Legislative Bulletin (quarterly); Our Heritage Newsletter (quarterly); Bibliographic Research and Resource Guide to the Hispanic Elderly; studies and brochures.

CHILDREN OF AGING PARENTS (CAPS)
(2761 Trenton Road, Levittown, PA 19056, 215-547-1070). Offers referrals, workshops, guidance, and support. 6 regional groups. Publications: Capsule Newsletter (irregular); Self-Help Manual; Instant Aging-Sensory Deprivation Manual; Guide to Selecting a Nursing Home; Starting a Self-Help Group for Caregivers of the Elderly; bibliographies.

GRAY PANTHERS
(311 South Juniper Street, Suite 601, Philadephia, PA 19107, 215-545-6555). Advises, catalyzes, and organizes local groups to address issues of their choosing; combats ageism against older adults and young people; maintains research file, information, and referral service. 100 local groups. Publications: The Network Newspaper (bimonthly); Organizing Manual; books.

NATIONAL ASSOCIATION FOR HOME CARE (NAHC)
(519 C Street, Washington, DC, 20002, 202-547-7424) Represents home health, hospice, and homemaker service providers; advocates for services; maintains list of home health care organizations. Publications: Caring Magazine (monthly); Homecare News (monthly).

NATIONAL ASSOCIATION OF MEDICAL EQUIPMENT
SUPPLIERS *(NAMES)* (618 S. Alfred Street, Alexandria, VA 22314, 703-836-6263). Represents suppliers of durable medical equipment and oxygen; supports legislation beneficial to the home health care industry. 43 regional groups. Publications: Names News (weekly); Washington Report (monthly); Membership Directory.

NATIONAL CAUCUS AND CENTER ON BLACK AGED (NCCBA)
(1424 K Street NW, Suite 500, Washington, DC 20005, 202-637-8400). Sponsors an employment program for older people; advocates legislation to improve the economic, social, and health status of low-income senior citizens. 45 local groups. Publications: Journal (quarterly); bulletins relating to the status of older Black Americans.

NATIONAL CONSUMERS LEAGUE (NCL)
(814 15th Street NW, Suite 516, Washington, DC 20005, 202-639-8140). Encourages citizen participation in government and industry decisions; semi-annual health care conference. 4

state groups. Publications: NCL Bulletin (bimonthly); Annual Consumer Report Card; guides and fact sheets.

NATIONAL COUNCIL OF SENIOR CITIZENS (NCSC)
(925 - 15th Street NW, Washington, DC 20005, (202) 347-8800). Provides nursing home information, maintains library on Medicare, supports action aiding senior citizens. Publication: Senior Citizen News (monthly).

THE NATIONAL COUNCIL ON THE AGING, INC. (NCOA)
(600 Maryland Avenue SW, West Wing 100, Washington, DC 20024, 202-479-1200). Promotes contact between people wanting to start caregiving programs and experts to advise them. Publications: Caregiver Support Groups; Guidelines for Practice; Supports for Family Caregivers of the Elderly; Respite Companion Program Model; State Support for Respite Care: Report of a Survey; Informal Supports: Summary of... Funded Research...; Ideabook on Caregiver Support Groups; Articles for Caregivers.

NATIONAL HOMECARING COUNCIL
(235 Park Avenue South, New York 10003, 212-674-4990). Guides communities in organizing & extending homemaker-home health services; distributes educational materials. Publications: Directory of Homemaker-Home Health Aide Services in the U.S.; All About Homecare: A Consumer's Guide.

NATIONAL HOSPICE ORGANIZATION (NHO)
(1901 N. Fort Myer Drive, Suite 307, Arlington, VA 22209). Research; standards; monitors legislation; provides information on local hospice programs. Publications: President's Letter (monthly); Newsletter (quarterly); Proceedings (annual); reports.

NATIONAL INDIAN COUNCIL ON AGING (NICOA)

(P.O. Box 2088, Albuquerque, NM 87103, 505-242-9505). Provides information on native Indian and Alaskan aging programs. Publications: Elder Voices (monthly); reports and monographs.

NATIONAL INSTITUTE ON ADULT DAYCARE (NIAD)

(c/o National Council on the Aging, 600 Maryland Ave. SW, W. Wing 100, Washington DC 20024, 202-479-1200). Promotes development of adult day care services; develops standards and guidelines; provides training; surveys state programs; lobbies for legislation. 10 regional groups. Publications: Adult Daycare Quarterly; Standards for Adult Daycare; Developing Adult Daycare: An Approach to Maintaining Independence for Impaired Older Persons.

NATIONAL PACIFIC/ASIAN RESOURCE CENTER ON AGING

(NP/ARCA) (Colorado Bldg, 1341 G St. NW, Suite 311, Washington, DC 20005, 202-393-7838). Promotes delivery of health and social services to elderly Pacific/Asians. 4 regional groups. Publications: Update Newsletter (bimonthly); National Community Service Directory: Pacific/Asian Elderly (biennial); Pacific/Asian Elderly: Bibliography; Proceedings of Pacific Asians: The Wisdom of Age; Guide to the Utilization of Family and Community Support Systems; medical handbook.

NATIONAL SHARED HOUSING RESOURCE CENTER (NSHRC)

(6344 Greene Street, Philadelphia, PA 19144, 215-848-1220). Provides information, education, technical assistance, and research on shared housing. 2 local groups. Publications: Shared Housing Quarterly; National Directory of Shared Housing Programs (irregular); National Policy Workshop on Shared Housing; Shared Housing: Findings and Recommendations; Homesharing Self-Help Guide; Planning Manual for Group Residences; Planning Manual for Match-Up Programs.

NATIONAL SUPPORT CENTER FOR FAMILIES OF THE AGING

(P.O. Box 245, Swarthmore, PA 19081, 215-544-5933). Aids family members responsible for an elderly person; aids those confronting their own aging; encourages formation of local support groups; helps families make decisions. Publications: Change Bulletin (quarterly); Help for Families of the Aging (workbook and cassettes); Directory of 62 Caregiver Support Programs.

OLDER WOMEN'S LEAGUE (OWL)

(730 11th Street NW, Suite 300, Washington, DC 20001, 202-783-6686). Provides leadership and advocacy for issues of concern to midlife and older women. 100 local groups. Publications: OWL OBSERVER (6 times/yr); A Model State Bill for Respite Care Legislation and a Model State Bill to Prevent the Spousal Impoverishment of Caregivers; Gray Papers (in-depth analysis of key issues: 'Til Death Do Us Part; Caregivers of Severely Disabled Husbands; Death and Dying: Staying in Control to the End of Our Lives; Health Care Financing and Midlife Women: A Sick System).

RETIRED PERSONS SERVICES (RPS)

(One Prince St., Alexandria, VA 22314, 703-684-0244). Provides mail-service prescription and nonprescription drugs, vitamins, and other health care items for members of AARP. 11 state locations for walk-in service.

SOCIETY FOR THE RIGHT TO DIE (SRD)

(250 W. 57th St., New York 10107, 212-246-6973). Provides information, appropriate right-to-die documents, and telephone referrals; committees include geriatrics and hospice. Publications: Newsletter (3/yr); Handbook of Will Legislation (annual).

Organizations for Help with Specific Diseases

ALZHEIMER'S DISEASE AND RELATED DISORDERS ASSOCIA-
TION (ADRDA) (70 East Lake Street, Chicago, IL 60601, 800-
621-0379, 312-853-3060). Works to develop family support
systems for relatives of victims; promotes research; provides
educational and awareness programs; represents affected population before government and social service agencies. 143
local groups. Publication: Newsletter (quarterly).

AMERICAN CANCER SOCIETY (ACS)
(90 Park Avenue, New York 10016, 212-599-8200). Sponsors
Reach to Recovery, CanSurmount, and I Can Cope; provides
special services to patients; supports research and education.
3,000 local groups; 58 regional groups. Publications: Cancer:
A Journal of the American Cancer Society (monthly); CA: A
Cancer Journal for Clinicians (bimonthly); Cancer News (3/yr);
World Smoking and Health (3/yr); Cancer Facts and Figures
(annual).

AMERICAN DIABETES ASSOCIATION (ADA)
(National Service Center, P.O. Box 25757, 1660 Duke Street,
Alexandria, VA 22313, 703-549-1500). Supports research
and education. 700 local groups; 62 regional groups. Publication: Forecast.

AMERICAN FOUNDATION FOR THE BLIND
(15 E. 16th Street, New York 10011, 212-620-2000). Records
talking books; maintains reference and lending library; develops special aids; sponsors workshops; participates in
legislative action. No local or regional groups. Publications:
Journal of Visual Impairment and Blindness (recorded and
printed; 10/yr); Newsletter (printed; quarterly); Long Care
News (printed; semiannual); Directory of Agencies Serving
the Blind and Visually Impaired in the U.S.; books, mono-

graphs, and pamphlets for blind people, professional workers, and the public.

AMERICAN HEART ASSOCIATION (AHA)

(7320 Greenville Avenue, Dallas, TX 75231, 214-750-5300). Supports research and education on cardiovascular diseases and stroke. Councils include Arteriosclerosis, Cardiopulmonary Diseases, Cardiovascular Nursing, Cardiovascular Radiology, Cardiovascular Surgery, Circulation, Epidemiology, High Blood Pressure Research, Kidney in Cardiovascular Disease, Stroke, Thrombosis. 55 regional groups. Publications: Circulation (monthly); Circulation Research (monthly); Modern Concepts of Cardiovascular Disease (monthly); Cardio-Vascular Nursing (bimonthly); Current Concepts of Cerebrovascular Disease-Stroke (bimonthly); Hypertension (bimonthly); Journal of Cerebral Circulation (bimonthly).

AMERICAN LUNG ASSOCIATION (ALA)

(1740 Broadway, New York 10019, 212-315-8700). Supports research and education. 82 local groups; 59 regional groups. Publications: American Review of Respiratory Diseases.

AMERICAN PARKINSON DISEASE ASSOCIATION (APDA)

(116 John Street, Suite 417, New York 10038, 800-223-2732, 212-732-9550). Subsidizes patient information and referral centers; funds research. 30 regional groups. Publications: Newsletter (semiannual); booklets.

AMERICAN SPEECH-LANGUAGE-HEARING ASSOCIATION

(ASHA) (10801 Rockville Pike, Rockville, MD 20852, 301-897-5700). Researches communication disorders and community needs for direct studies. No local groups. Publications: ASHA (monthly); Journal of Speech and Hearing Disorders (quarterly); Journal of Speech and Hearing Research (quarterly); Language, Speech, and Hearing Services in Schools (quarterly); Guide to Professional Services in Speech-Language Pathology and Audiology; monographs; reports.

AMYOTROPHIC LATERAL SCLEROSIS (ALS) ASSOCIATION
(15300 Ventura Blvd., Suite 315, Sherman Oaks, CA 91403, 818-990-2151). Offers help, information, and referrals to patients and their families. 12 local groups; 10 regional groups. Publications: The ALS Association Newsletter (quarterly); fact sheets and pamphlets on symptomatic treatment.

ARTHRITIS FOUNDATION (RHEUMATIC DISEASES)
(3400 Peachtree Rd. NE, Atlanta, GA 30326, 404-266-0795). Provides information to the lay public; presents annual writing awards. 71 local groups. Publications: Arthritis & Rheumatism (monthly); Bulletin on Rheumatic Diseases (9/yr); National Arthritis News (quarterly); Index of Rheumatology (annual).

ASSOCIATION FOR BRAIN TUMOR RESEARCH (ABTR)
(6232 N. Pulaski Road, Suite 400, Chicago, IL 60646, 312-286-5571). Supports research and patient education. No local groups. Publications: Message Line (annual); A Primer of Brain Tumors; Treatment of Brain Tumors; pamphlets.

HUNTINGTON'S DISEASE FOUNDATION OF AMERICA (HDFA)
(250 W. 57th Street, Suite 2016, New York, NY 10107, 212-757-0443). Supports research and patient education; crisis intervention; lending library of audiovisual materials. 51 local groups; 15 regional groups. Publications: Newsletter (3/yr); Annual Report; booklets and pamphlets.

EPILEPSY FOUNDATION OF AMERICA
(4251 Garden City Drive, Landover, MD 20785, 301-459-3700). Offers referrals, assistance, and counseling for patients and their families; provides low-cost pharmacy program. 85 regional groups. Publications: National Spokesman Newspa-

per (monthly); Epilepsy Advances Newsletter (quarterly); pamphlets; audio/visual material.

NATIONAL ASSOCIATION OF THE DEAF (NAD)

(814 Thayer Ave., Silver Spring, MD 20910, 301-587-1788). Offers information on deafness; promotes legislation; protects civil rights; supports vocational training, rehabilitative services, educational opportunities, and mental health services; Metro-Washington-area training for under-educated and disadvantaged deaf. 50 regional groups. Publications: Broadcaster Newspaper (11/yr); Deaf American Magazine (quarterly); textbooks on American sign language and other systems of manual communication; books on all aspects of deafness.

NATIONAL COUNCIL ON ALCOHOLISM (NCA)

(12 W. 21st St., New York 10010, 212-206-6770). Provides information and programs on alcoholism; coordinates telephone hotlines in many communities. 184 local groups. Publications: pamphlets, books, and catalogues on aspects of alcoholism and its treatment.

NATIONAL HEAD INJURY FOUNDATION (NHIF)

(P.O. Box 567, Framingham, MA 01701, 617-879-7473). Provides telephone information to those who suffered head injuries and their families, including care facilities, legal rights, and support groups. 23 regional groups. Publications: NHIF Newsletter (quarterly); Annual Report; Resource Directory (annual).

NATIONAL MULTIPLE SCLEROSIS SOCIETY (NMSS)

(205 East 42nd St., New York 01017, 212-986-3240. Provides services to people with MS and related diseases and their families. 139 local groups; 5 regional groups. Publications: Inside MS (quarterly); Therapeutic Claims in Multiple Sclerosis; Research on Multiple Sclerosis; Maximizing Your Health.

NATIONAL PARKINSON FOUNDATION (NPF)

(1501 NW Ninth Ave., Miami, FL 33136, 305-576-6666). Sponsors regional patient self-support groups; distributes educational literature; supports National Parkinson Institute to treat patients. Publication: Newsletter (quarterly).

Books and Pamphlets

Many of these books will be available at your local library or bookstore. If they are not, libraries can often get them through inter-library loan. Some college, hospital, and health maintenance libraries are open to the public. You may also order books directly from the publisher. Your local library can supply the publisher's address. Ordering through a mail order book supplier by credit card may be a bit more expensive (an example is Book Call, 1-800-255-2665).

Caregiving Guides

Caregiving: Helping an Aging Loved One, by Jo Horne (Prospect, IL: AARP Publications, Scott-Foresman, 1985), 319 p.

Thorough hands-on information by an adult day care center administrator, including a Caregiver's Bill of Rights, a list of State Units on Aging, and a reading list.

Caresharing: How to Relate to the Frail Elderly, edited by Katherine V. Gray (Minneapolis, MN: Ebenezer Center for Aging and Human Development, 1984), 80 p.

Based on the belief that people needing care can be equal partners in a cooperative effort involving all the caresharing family members, loved ones, friends, aides, and professionals.

A Guide to Dying at Home, by Deborah Duda (Santa Fe, NM: John Muir Press, 1982).

With examples from personal experience, suggests preparations for returning from the hospital, making the patient comfortable, utilizing medical, financial, and legal services, dealing
with feelings, preparing for death, planning for burial, grieving
and mourning.

*The Healing Family: The Simonton Approach for Families Facing
Illness*, by Stephanie Matthews Simonton and Robert L. Shook
(New York: Bantam, 1984), 288 p.

Not specific to age, disease, or home care, this exploration of
emotional relationships among patients, families, and caregivers offers techniques for managing stress, pain, and fear as
well as communicating feelings.

Home Care: An Alternative to the Nursing Home, by Florine
DeFresne (Elgin, IL: Brethren Press, 1983), 127 p.

A complete how-to guide written by a caregiver.

Home Care for the Elderly, by Julie Trocchio (Boston, MA: CBI
Publishing, 1981), 176 p.

By a registered nurse, guidelines for home care decisions and
basics of home nursing for families or aides with selected list
of other nursing and general resources.

*Home Health Care: A Complete Guide for Patients and Their Fam-
ilies*, by Jo Ann Friedman (New York: Norton, 1986), 589 p.

Emphasizes daily living, nursing, individual health problems,
insurance and organization methods; gives addresses of state
Adult Day Care Associations and community service providers.

The Home Health Care Solution: A Complete Consumer Guide, by
Janet Zhun Nassif (New York: Harper & Row, 1985), 416 p.

How to obtain medical equipment, supplies, personnel, services, insurance, and other resources for the least cost; detailed checklists; addresses of state and national homecare-related organizations.

The Loss of Self: A Family Resource for the Care of Alzheimer's Disease and Related Disorders, by Donna Cohen and Carl Eisdorfer (New York: Norton, 1986), 381 p.

Guidelines for developing coping strategies; personal accounts in the form of dialogues, interviews, and letters illustrate an almost predictable series of crises; places individual situations in a societal context.

Managing Incontinence: A Guide to Living with the Loss of Bladder Control, edited by Cheryle B. Gartley (Ottawa, IL: Jameson Books, 1985), 240 p.

Presents personal experiences, explores physical and attitudinal aspects, and evaluates products and devices.

Our Aging Parents: A Practical Guide to Eldercare, edited by Colette Browne and Robert Onzuka-Anderson (Honolulu, HI: University of Hawaii Press, 1985), 305 p.

Sensible treatment of aging and the family, health concerns, special problems of the dependent elderly, and an especially sensitive discussion of depression.

Taking Care: A Self-Help Guide for Coping with an Elderly, Chronically Ill, or Disabled Relative, by Jill Watt and Ann Calder (Seattle, WA: Self-Counsel Press, 1986), 128 p.

Treats attitudes, living arrangements, self-care, specific remedies and problem areas; provides worksheets to help organize caretaking tasks.

Taking Care: Supporting Older People and Their Families, by Nancy Hooyman and Wendy Lustbader (New York: Free Press, 1986), 322 p.

This thorough guide includes sections on practical and emotional aspects of long-distance caregiving; ethnic differences; lesbian and gay issues; strategies for enlarging the caregiving group; alternative living situations, and extending care into the nursing home; annotated references.

The 36-Hour Day: A Family Guide to Caring for Persons with Alzheimer's Disease, Related Dementing Illnesses and Memory Loss in Later Life, by Nancy L. Mace and Peter V. Rabins (Baltimore, MD: Johns Hopkins Univ. Press, 1981), 253 p.

Includes general and specific treatment of special problems caused by mental deterioration, protection from injury, coping with feelings and tensions, importance of durable power of attorney.

Understanding "Senility": A Layperson's Guide, by Virginia Fraser & Susan M. Thornton (Buffalo, NY: Prometheus, 1987), 103 p.

Brief, down-to-earth information to help in family management and decision-making with basic check-lists and thoughts about the nursing home alternative.

We Are Not Alone: Learning to Live with Chronic Illness, by Sefra Kobrin Pitzele (Minneapolis, MN: Thompson, 1985), 320 p.

Begins earlier in the process than many other books; puts the patient in charge; discusses diagnosis, grieving losses, and communication skills; lists equipment suppliers.

Who Cares? Helpful Hints for Those Who Care for a Dependent Older Person at Home, by The Andrus Volunteers Publication Committee (Los Angeles, CA: University of Southern California, 1985), 72 p.

Cheerful, down-to-earth, and carefully chosen tips and resources, includes Caregiver Bill of Rights, model programs, and information about durable power of attorney for health care.

Public Affairs Pamphlets (381 Park Ave., So., New York 10016). Free lists are available of the many short, informative pamphlets for sale ($1 each). Topics include "After 65: Resources for Self-Reliance" (#501); "Home Health Care: When a Patient Leaves the Hospital" (#560); and "The Right to Die with Dignity" (# 587A), among many others.

Guides by physicians provide helpful advice from a medical rather than a hands-on caregiver perspective. Several recent ones are *Caring for an Elderly Relative: A Guide to Home Care*, by Keith M. Thompson (New York: Prentice Hall, 1986), 128 p.; *Caring for Your Aging Parents: A Concerned Complete Guide for Children of the Elderly*, by Robert R. Cadmus (Englewood Cliffs, NJ: Prentice Hall, 1984), 253 p.; and *Growing Old: A Handbook for You and Your Aging Parent*, by David A. Tombs (New York: Viking, 1984), 416 p.

Denominational guides reflect particular religious perspectives. Several well-known ones are *The Aging Parent: A Guide for Program Planners*, by the American Jewish Committee (New York: Institute of Human Relations, 1980), 50 p.; *A Guide to Caring for and Coping with Aging Parents* (Protestant), (Nashville, TN: Thomas Nelson, 1981); *Understanding Aging Parents* (Protestant), by Andrew D. and Judith L. Lester (Philadelphia, PA: Westminster Press, 1980), 120 p.; and *Your Aging Parents* (Catholic), by John Deedy (Chicago, IL: Thomas More Press, 1984), 186 p.

Personal Accounts

Reading accounts of other caregivers' experiences, processes, and solutions to problems can provide emotional and practical support and inspiration.

Caring for an Aging Parent: Have I Done All I Can? by Avis Jane Ball (Buffalo, NY: Prometheus, 1986), 134 p.

A daughter undertakes the care of her deteriorating father with responsibility, courage, love, and faith; poignantly details her pilgrimage through the ups and downs of loss, fear, hope, anger, and resentment.

Caring: A Daughter's Story, by Diane Ruben (New York: Holt, Rinehart & Winston, 1982), 176 p.

A daughter's care and concern for two ailing parents entails the maturation of the relationship with her mother as well as ambivalent feelings about caregiving.

Final Payments, by Mary Gordon (New York: Ballantine, 1978), 320 p.

A powerful novel about a woman's isolation as she cares for her father for ten years and about the challenges of her re-entry into social relationships and paid employment after her father's death.

Handle With Care: A Question of Alzheimer's, by Dorothy S. Brown (Buffalo, NY: Prometheus, 1985), 120 p.

A sensitive and loving portrayal of the difficulties and trauma of caring for a mother suffering from the progressive deterioration of her mental faculties; relates feelings and discusses symptoms, options for care, and financial and legal issues.

The Healing Heart: Antidotes to Panic and Helplessness (New York: Norton, 1983) 240 p., and *Anatomy of an Illness as Perceived by the Patient* (New York: Bantam, 1981), 176 p.

Both by Norman Cousins, emphasize humor and optimism and insist on the patient as a partner with physicians and caregivers in combatting serious illness.

In Sunshine and Shadow, edited by Judy Oliver (Sherman Oaks, CA: Amyotrophic Lateral Sclerosis Association, 1986), 171 p.

Moving essays and reminiscences by patients and family members of patients with Amyotrophic Lateral Sclerosis (ALS).

Living with Alzheimer's: Ruth's Story, by Art Danforth (Falls Church, VA: Prestige Press, P.O. Box 2608, 22042), 1986.

A husband's frank account of daily life as he coped with his wife's physical and mental deterioration; expresses the fear and concern as well as the anger and guilt.

The Summer of the Great-Grandmother, by Madeline L'Engle (New York: Seabury, 1980), 246 p.

A moving account of a daughter's experience in caring for her mother and preparing for her mother's death.

A Reckoning, by May Sarton (New York: Norton, 1981), 254 p.

Novel of a woman with inoperable cancer who decides to die in her own way, using illness as a final journey during which she must reckon up her life.

The Rest of My Life, by Laura Russell Hunter with Polly Memhard (Riverside, CT: Growing Pains Press, 1981), 112 p.

An octogenarian's astute and humorous account of her final years as a nursing home resident; suggests caresharing conditions that encourage self-determination during aging, illness, and dying.

The Twilight Years, by Sawako Ariyoshi (New York: Kodansha, 1984), 216 p.

Translated from the Japanese by Mildred Tahara, a novel about a middle-aged daughter-in-law caring for a senile old man.

Health Care Decisions

When home care must be supplemented by community services or replaced by institutional care, decision-making can be facilitated by some of the titles listed below.

Alzheimers: *Family Survival Handbook: A Guide to the Financial, Legal and Social Problems of Brain-Damaged Adults* (San Francisco, CA: Family Survival Project, free).

Board and Care: *A Home Away From Home: Consumer Information on Board and Care Homes* (Wash., DC: AARP, 1986).

Home Health Care: *A Consumer's Guide to Home Health Care* (Washington, DC: National Consumers League); *How to Select a Home Care Agency* (Washington, DC: National Association for Home Care).

Life-Care: *A Consumer Guide to Life-Care Communities* (Washington, DC: National Consumers League, 1986).

Living Wills: The Society for the Right to Die (250 W. 57th Street, Suite 323, New York 10107) provides free documents conforming to each state's law; Concern for Dying (250 W. 57th

Street, Room 831, New York 10019) offers free information and model documents.

Nursing Homes: *Choosing a Nursing Home: A Guidebook for Families* (Seattle, WA: University of Washington Press, 1985, rev. ed.), 110 p.; *How to Select a Nursing Home* (Wash., DC: U.S. Dept. of Health and Human Services, 1980), 55 p.; *When Love Gets Tough: The Nursing Home Decision* (Hereford, TX: In-Sight Books, 1983, rev. ed.), 62 p.; *You, Your Parent, and the Nursing Home* (Buffalo, NY: Prometheus, 1986), 174 p.

Terminal Illness: *Choices for People Who Have a Terminal Illness, Their Families, and Their Caregivers* (Toronto: NC Press, 1986), 194 p. Personal perspectives of dying people, families, & caregivers; encourages teamwork; detailed, practical questions to ask, legal rights, wills, pain and symptom control, palliative & hospice care, right to die, funeral preparations.

Starting a Support Group or Service Program

Solutions to the lack of supportive services are to join or form self-help groups or to participate in the development of needed services. Some of the materials below might be helpful.

Developing Respite Services for the Elderly, by Rhonda J.V. Montgomery and Joyce Prothero (Seattle, WA: University of Washington Press, 1986), 82 p.

Family Caregivers and Dependent Elderly: Minimizing Stress and Maximizing Independence, by Dianne Springer and Timothy H. Brubaker (Beverly Hills, CA: Sage, 1984), 159 p.

Family Seminars for Caregiving: A Facilitator's Guidebook (Seattle, WA: University of Washington Press).

Ideabook on Caregiver Support Groups: Findings of a Survey and National Directory (Washington, DC: National Council on the Aging, 1985), 40 p.

In Support of Caregivers: Materials for Planning and Conducting Educational Workshops (Madison, WI: Vocational Studies Center, University of Wisconsin-Madison).

Leading Self-Help Groups, by Lucretia Mallory (New York: Family Service Association of America, 1984), 72 p.

Practical Help: Caring for an Elderly Person in the Community, an informal caregiver's curriculum (Albany, NY: New York State Office for the Aging, 1982).

Respite Companion Program Model, by Lorraine Lidoff (Washington, DC: National Council on the Aging, 1983), 57 p.

Self-Care and Self-Help Groups for the Elderly: A Directory (Washington, DC: US National Institute on Aging, 1984), 128 p.

Starting a Self-Help Group for Caregivers of the Elderly (Levittown, PA: Children of Aging Parents, 1984).

Support Groups for Caregivers of the Aged: A Training Manual for Facilitators (NY: Community Service Society, 1981), 72 p.

Partnership With Society

If you are doing advocacy for support services, these will provide useful analysis and data.

Caregivers of the Frail Elderly: A National Profile, a report prepared for the National Center for Health Services Research, documents how many women caregivers must quit their jobs to care for a disabled relative (Rockville, MD: NCHSR Publications, 1986, free).

The Chronically Limited Elderly: The Case for a National Policy for In-Home and Supportive Community-Based Services, by Howard A. Palley & Julianne S. Oktay (NY: Haworth, 1983), 142 p.

An overview of long-term care policy equity, adequacy, and public accountability; legislative proposals; international comparisons.

Developments in Aging. Annual report giving the latest data about the aging population, government responsibility, and national policy needs (Washington, DC 20510: U.S. Senate Special Committee on Aging).

Exploding the Myths: Caregiving in America. A study by the Subcommittee on Human Services of the Select Committee on Aging, House of Representatives, January 1987. Publication 99-661 U.S. Government Printing Office, may be requested from the House Committee on Aging, Washington, DC 20515.

Labour of Love: Women, Work, and Caring, edited by Janet Finch and Dulcie Groves (Boston: Routledge & Kegan Paul, 1983), 192 p.

A political analysis of caregiving and the ways in which society fails to acknowledge the tensions between women's economic independence and their responsibilities as caregivers.

Long Term Care of the Elderly: Public Policy Issues, by Charlene Harrington, Robert J. Newcomer, Carroll L. Estes and Associates from the Institute for Health & Aging, University of California at San Francisco (Beverly Hills, CA: Sage, 1985), 280 p.

Explores the tension between increasing needs and shrinking resources; critiques policy shifts; and recommends reforms.

Respite Care: Supporting Families of Developmentally Disabled Persons, by Shirley Cohen and Rachel D. Warren (Winthrop, MA: Professional Editorial Service, 1985), 242 p.

Provides practice and research-based arguments for the need of respite care provision; outlines training, legal, and fiscal guidelines for programs; and gives models.

Shared Obligations: Public Policy Influences on Family Care for the Elderly, by Brian Burwell (Baltimore, MD: U.S. Health Care Financing Administration, 1986).

Examines incentives and disincentives by government for informal caregiving.

Ties That Bind: The Interdependence of Generations, by Eric Kingson (Cabin John, MD: Seven Locks Press, 1986), 208 p.

Presents policy choices from the perspective of the Gerontological Society of America; analyzes existing arrangements for family caregiving and the argument that the elderly are getting more than their share of health resources.

NOTES

CHAPTER 1

Page 21: Statistics in the first few paragraphs are drawn from "Who Cares? Semographic Trends Challenge Family Care for the Elderly," by Alice T. Day. Occasional Paper No. 9, published by the Population Reference Bureau, Inc., Washington, D.C., September 1985, and "Exploding the Myths: Caregiving in America." Study of the Subcommittee on Human Services of the House Select Committee on Aging. Washington, D.C.: U.S. Government Printing Office, 1987.

CHAPTER 2

Pages 42 and page 44: The figures of half the caregivers saying caregiving is emotionally diffcult and that their social life has been limited are drawn from "Exploding the Myths: Caregiving in America," A Study by the Subcommittee on Human Services, House Select Committee on Aging, U.S. Government Printing Office #99-611, 1987.

CHAPTER 3

Page 69: Strictly speaking Blue Cross, Blue Shield, and Health Maintenance Organizations (HMOs, like the Kaiser system) are *not* health insurance. Only commercial carriers, such as Mutual of Omaha, Prudential and Hartford, qualify as true health insurance. However, since the differences are largely technical and administrative, we have considered them here together.

CHAPTER 6

Pages 105 and 106: Statistics are taken from "Who Cares? Demographic Trends Challenge Family Care for the Elderly." By Alice T. Day, Washington, D.C.: Population Reference Bureau, ninth paper in a series entitled *Population Trends and Public Policy*, 1985.

Page 106: Information on the Travelers survey is drawn from a news summary dated December 12, 1985, issues by Alan R. Fletcher, Administrator, Public Relations, The Travelers, One Tower Square, Hartford, CT 06183-1060.

Page 111: Quote attributed to the National Association of State Units on Aging is taken from page 6 of "A Synthesis of Issues and Findings on Primary Caregivers: Support Systems," report prepared by NASUA for the Office of Human Development Services, DHHS, June, 1984, Washington, D.C.

Pages 117 and 118: Facts cited about minority elderly having more chronic diseases and disabilties at younger ages, and a history that leads to their need for care are taken from Robert G. Robinson and Henrik L. Blum, "Evidence Supporting a General System or Ecologic View of Health," in *Expanding Health Care Horizons*, by Henrik L. Blum, Oakland, 1983: Third Party Publishing Co.

Page 117: Blacks and Hispanics underrepresented in nursing homes, from Bruce G. Vladeck, *Unloving Care: The Nursing Home Tragedy*, New York: Basic Books, 1980.

Pages 124 and 125: Margaret's comments on caring for Bobbi are quoted from "Caring for Bobbi: An Incredible Gift," by Margaret Hackman and Monica Raymond, *Sojourner*, December, 1986.

Pages 125 and 126: The story of Dorothy Healy is taken from the Los Angeles Herald Examiner, May 14, 1984, page A-13.

CHAPTER 8

Page 154: A copy of the Older Women's League Model State Bill for Respite Care is available from Older Women's League, 730 11th Street, NW, Suite 300, Washington, DC 20001.

Page 157: A copy of the Older Women's League Model State Bill on Preventing the Impoverishment of Caregiving Spouses is available from Older Women's League, 730 11th Street, Suite 300, Washington, DC 20001.

Page 162: A copy of the Older Women's League State Bill on Preventing Nursing Home Discrimination Against Medicaid Patients is available from Older Women's League, 730 11th St., N.W., Suite 300 Washington, DC 20001.

CHAPTER 9

Page 179: Barbara Ehrenreich and Dierdre English, *For Her Own Good: 150 Years of the Experts Advice to Women.* Anchor Books, 1979, pages 20-26.